An Orange Tree Theatre, Octa
co-pro

TESTMATCH

by Kate Attwell

Testmatch was workshopped at JAW: A Playwrights Festival
produced by Portland Center Stage.
Originally produced by American Conservatory Theater,
San Francisco, 24 October 2019
Pam McKinnon, Artistic Director – Jennifer Bielstein, Executive
Director.

The UK premiere was first performed on 20 April 2024
at the Orange Tree Theatre, Richmond.

CAST

India 2 / Daanya — **Aiyana Bartlett**
India 1 / Messenger — **Aarushi Riya Ganju**
England 3 / Two — **Haylie Jones**
India 3 / Abhi — **Tanya Katyal**
England 1 / One — **Bea Svistunenko**
England 2 / Memsahib — **Mia Turner**

CREATIVES AND PRODUCTION TEAM

Writer — **Kate Attwell**
Director — **Diane Page**
Designer — **Cat Fuller**
Lighting Designer — **Rajiv Pattani**
Composer & Sound Designer — **Simon Slater**

Casting Director — **Matilda James CDG**
Costume Supervisor — **Agata Odolczyk**
Fight & Intimacy Director — **Ruth Cooper-Brown** for RC Annie
Production LX — **Matt Carnazza**
Assistant Director — **Anna Sharp**
Wigs provided by — **Chris Smyth**

Production Manager — **Lisa Hood**
Company Stage Manager — **Jenny Skivens**
Deputy Stage Manager — **Judith Volk**
Assistant Stage Manager — **Charlotte Smith-Barker**
Production & Rehearsal Photography — **Helen Murray**

Thanks to
Eleanor Oldroyd, Daniel Burke, Anna Charlesworth, Jatinder Verma MBE, Kat Wells.

Aiyana Bartlett
India 2 and Daanya

Testmatch marks Aiyana's
UK theatre debut.

Theatre credits include *A Hundred
Words for Snow* (Gothenburg
English Studio Theatre).

Aiyana trained at the Oxford
School of Drama.

Aarushi Riya Ganju
India 1 and Messenger

Theatre credits include *The Ghost
of Thomas Kempe* (reading; RSC);
Unlocking Canons House (Attic
Theatre); *Roobaroo* (reading; The
Space); *Henry VIII* (The Show
Must Go Online).

Radio credits include *Make
Death Love Me: Antony and
Cleopatra Reimagined*.

Television credits include *Doctors*
and *3 Body Problem*.

Aarushi trained at Drama
Centre London.

This is her UK professional
stage debut.

Haylie Jones
England 3 and Two

Theatre credits include *Lear* (Hope Mill Theatre, Shakespeare North Playhouse); *Romeo and Juliet*, *Little Women*, *Stig of the Dump* (Grosvenor Park Open Air Theatre); and *A Brew, A Terrace and the 184* (Oldham Coliseum Theatre).

Television credits include *Blind Spot*, *Stay Close*, *Coronation Street* and *The Cup*.

Film credits include *Wanderland* and *Public House*.

Haylie trained at the Manchester School of Acting.

Tanya Katyal
India 3 and Abhi

Theatre credits include *The Empress* (RSC).

Television credits include *Eternally Confused* and *Eager For Love*.

Tanya trained at Royal Welsh College of Music and Drama.

Bea Svistunenko
England 1 and One

Theatre credits include *The Tempest* (Shakespeare's Globe); *Macbeth*, *Romeo and Juliet* (Guildford Shakespeare Company); and *A Very Expensive Poison* (The Old Vic).

Television credits include *3 Body Problem*, *I Hate Suzie Too*, *Litvinenko* and *Industry*.

Bea has recently starred alongside Olivia Colman and Adrian Lester in *Before Our Eyes* (Amnesty UK Campaign).

Bea trained at RADA.

Mia Turner
England 2 and Memsahib

Theatre credits include *Boys* (Tabard Theatre).

Mia trained at Arts Ed.

Kate Attwell
Writer

Kate Attwell is a playwright, screenwriter, and devised theatremaker who regularly works between London and New York. Recent productions include *Big Data* at A.C.T.'s Toni Rembe Theatre directed by Pam McKinnon and starring Tony Winner BD Wong.

Testmatch premiered at A.C.T. in 2019, also directed by Pam MacKinnon and was an L. Arnold Weissberger New Play Award finalist. Her play *Jesus in Manhattan* anchored Ensemble Studio Theater's Marathon Series that same year, and she premiered *Demonstrating the Imaginary Body* at the 2016 Under the Radar festival and later at REDCAT.

Kate is currently working on commissions for Playwrights Horizons, Yale Rep, Manhattan Theatre Club and A.C.T. She won the Digital Culture Award, Digital Inclusion in 2022 for her short film, *Stile*, was a member of Ars Nova's PlayGroup, Page 73's Interstate 73 Writers' Group, and The Public Theater's Devised Theater Working Group. Her plays have been developed and seen at A.C.T., Playwrights Horizons, Yale Rep, Portland Center Stage, New York Theatre Workshop, The Bushwick Starr, CalArts, and The Public Theater (Under the Radar).

She holds a BA in Performance from The University of Bristol and an MFA from Yale University.

Diane Page
Director

Diane Page returns to the Orange Tree for a third time, following revered productions of Dael Orlandersmith's *Yellowman* in 2022, and as the 2021 JMK Award winner, directing Athol Fugard's *Statements After an Arrest Under the Immorality Act*. She is also an Associate Artist at the Orange Tree.

Other directing credits include: *The Tempest*, *Julius Caesar* (Shakespeare's Globe); *Lost and Found* (Royal Opera House) and *Out West* (co-director, Lyric Hammersmith Theatre).

Training: BA in Theatre and Drama Studies (First Class Hons.) and MFA Theatre Directing, both at Birkbeck College.

Cat Fuller
Designer

Cat Fuller has an MA in Performance Design from Bristol Old Vic Theatre School. In 2021, Cat was named a recipient of the Linbury Prize and was also awarded the John Elvery Prize for Excellence in Stage Design.

Her recent work as set and costume designer includes: *Scarlet Sunday* (Omnibus Theatre); *Owners* (Jermyn Street Theatre); *Flies* (Shoreditch Town Hall); *Snail* (VAULT 2023); *The Sweet Science of Bruising* (The Egg, Theatre Royal Bath); *Romeo and Juliet* (Weston Studio, Bristol Old Vic).

Work as set designer includes *The Three Seagulls* (Bristol Old Vic) and *Falling in Love Again* (The King's Head).

Her work as Associate Designer for Anna Fleischle includes: *The Time Traveller's Wife: The Musical* (Apollo Theatre London and Chester Storyhouse); *A Christmas Carol* (Finnish National Opera and Ballet); *Home I'm Darling* (UK Tour) and *Much Ado About Nothing* (National Theatre); and for Katie Sykes: *If You Fall* (Theatre Ad Infinitum).

Rajiv Pattani
Lighting Designer

Rajiv graduated from LAMDA in 2014 with qualifications in Stage Management and Technical Theatre.

Recent credits include: *Count Me In* (Leeds Playhouse); *10 Nights* (Omnibus/Tour); *Bonfire* (Derby Theatre/Sheffield Theatre/Nonsuch); *High Times and Dirty Monsters* (20 Stories High/Graeae/Liverpool Everyman/LEEDS 2023/Tour); *Strategic Love Play* (Paines Plough Roundabout/Tour); *Zoe's Peculiar Journey Through Time* (Southbank Centre and Tour); *£1 Thursdays* (Finborough Theatre); *The Garden of Words* (Park200); *Sorry, You're Not a Winner* (Paines Plough Tour); *Hairy, Let's Build!* (Polka Theatre); *The Flood* (Queen's Theatre Hornchurch); *SMOKE* (Southwark Playhouse/3 heart canvas); *Yellowfin* (Southwark Playhouse); *Kabul Goes Pop: Music Television Afghanistan*, *Alice in Wonderland* (Poltergeist Theatre Company/Brixton House); *Yellowman*, *Statements After an Arrest Under the Immortality Act*, *OUTSIDE* (Orange Tree Theatre); *Supernova* (also Tour), *Wolfie* (Theatre 503); *Mog the Forgetful Cat*, *Winners* (Wardrobe Ensemble); *Pilgrims* (Guildhall School of Music and Drama); *Final Farewell*, *Dawaat* (Tara Theatre); *Hunger* (Arcola); *Dirty Crusty* (Yard Theatre); *Dismantle This Room* (Royal Court Downstairs); *Nassim* (also Edinburgh Traverse/International Tour), *Babylon Beyond Borders*, *Leave Taking*, *Ramona Tells Jim* (Bush Theatre).

Simon Slater
Composer & Sound Designer

Simon is an Olivier nominated composer and has composed original music for over 400 theatre, film, television and radio productions. Recent theatre: the award-winning *Constellations* (West End, Royal Court New York and nominated for an Olivier); *Private Lives* and *Europe* (Donmar Warehouse); *Wilko* (Queen's Theatre Hornchuch); *Love Love Love*, *Out West* (Lyric Theatre); *Amadeus* (National Theatre, 2017 and 2018); *Jane Eyre* (Stephen Joseph Theatre Scarborough); *Killology* – winner of an Olivier 2018 (Sherman/Royal Court); *Carmen Disruption* (Almeida), *The Tempest*, *Julius Caesar*, *Tis Pity She's a Whore*, *The Broken Heart*, *A Winter's Tale*, *King Lear* (Shakespeare's Globe and Sam Wanamaker); *Henry V*, *Julius Caesar*, *Macbeth*, *Romeo and Juliet* (RSC); *The Deep Blue Sea*, *Death of a Salesman*, *The Grouch* (Leeds Playhouse).

Simon is an Associate Artist at the Stephen Joseph Theatre Scarborough where he has composed for many productions including *The 39 Steps*, *Brief Encounter*, *Little Voice*, *A Comedy of Errors*. TV and film include scores for *Holby City*, *Dalziel and Pasco*, *Crimes of Christine Keeler*, *Traitors*, *My One and Only*, *Inquisition*, and the recent feature *And Then Come the Nightjars*. As a performer Simon is a regular face on TV and in theatre and audiobooks, including awards for his narration of *Wolf Hall* and his one man show, *Bloodshot* which he has performed all over the world. Recently his scores for *Black Water*, *A Ghastly Mistake*, *Silos* can be heard on BBC Radio 3 and Radio 4.

Matilda James CDG
Casting Director

Originally from Cornwall, Matilda works in casting for theatre, screen, and games. As casting director at Shakespeare's Globe from 2012-2017, she cast over 50 shows for the Globe and Sam Wanamaker Playhouse.

A founding member of the Murmuration, a women-led theatre & arts producing collective, her recent collaborations include work with the Barbican; York Theatre Royal and Kyiv City Ballet; #Merky Films; and Citizens of the World, the UK's leading choir for people seeking sanctuary and asylum.

Recent casting for theatre includes: *The House Party* (Chichester Festival Theatre/ Headlong); *A Child of Science* (Bristol Old Vic); *Uncle Vanya* (Orange Tree); *QUIZ* (Wessex Grove/JCTP); *2.22 A Ghost Story* (West End and on tour); *Family Tree* (Actors Touring Company/ Belgrade Theatre Coventry/ Brixton House); *Gin Craze!* (Northampton Royal & Derngate/ English Touring Theatre).

Film includes: *Portraits of Dangerous Women*, *Benjamin* and *Pond Life*.

Agata Odolczyk

Costume Supervisor

Theatre includes: Set and Costume Designer for *Conspiracy of Orphans* (Tramshed/Gothenburg Fringe/Created a Monster Theatre); Costume Supervisor for *Owners* (Jermyn Street Theatre); Costume Breakdown Artist for *Treason The Musical* (Alexandra Palace Theatre, The London Palladium).

Film includes (as Assistant Costume Designer): *Kleks Academy* (2023); *Republika Dzieci* (2021).

Short film includes (as Costume Designer): *Magnetic* (2022); *Back Up* (2021); *Esmeralda* (2020).

Agata trained in design at Royal Central School of Speech and Drama, London. She is based between London and Warsaw, working across performance, film and visual art.

Ruth Cooper-Brown

of Rc-Annie Ltd
Fight & Intimacy Director

Rc-Annie Ltd, established in 2005 by Rachel Bown-Williams and Ruth Cooper-Brown, is the UK's leading Dramatic Violence and Intimacy Company.

Theatre credits include: *The Duchess of Malfi*, *A Midsummer Night's Dream*, *The Tempest*, *Hakawatis*, *Midsummer Mechanicals*, *I, Joan*, *Henry VIII*, *Romeo and Juliet*, *Macbeth*, *Emilia*, *Othello*, *Boudica*, *Lions and Tigers*, *Much Ado About Nothing*, *Twelfth Night* (Shakespeare's Globe); *A Midsummer Night's Dream*, *The Empress*, *Julius Caesar*, *Richard III*, *Henry VI: Rebellion*, *The Wars of the Roses*, *King John*, *Measure for Measure*, *The Taming of the Shrew*, *Tartuffe*, *The Duchess of Malfi* (Royal Shakespeare Company); *Bronco Billy* (Charing Cross Theatre); *Macbeth* (Donmar Warehouse); *Minority Report* (Nottingham Playhouse); *Great Expectations* (Royal Exchange Manchester); *The Boys from the Blackstuff* (Liverpool Royal Court/Stockroom); *The Pillowman* (Duke of York Theatre); *It's Headed Straight Towards Us* (The Park Theatre); *Linck & Mülhahn*, *'Night Mother* (Hampstead Theatre); *Noises Off* (Theatre Royal Bath/West End); *Oklahoma* (Young Vic/West End); *Newsies* (Wesley Troubadour); *Baghdaddy* (Royal Court Theatre); *James IV* (Raw Material/Edinburgh Festival Theatre); *Never Have I Ever*; *Crazy for You*, *The Taxidermist's Daughter*, *Plenty* (Chichester Festival Theatre); *As You Like It* (CBBC and Shakespeare's Globe); *The Scandal at Mayerling* (Scottish Ballet); *Theodora* (Royal Opera House); *The Father and the Assassin*, *The Welkin*, *Three Sisters*, *Anna*, *When We Have Sufficiently Tortured Each Other*, *Peter Pan*, *The Threepenny Opera*, *The James Plays* (co-production with National Theatre of Scotland/Edinburgh International Festival); *Cleansed* (National Theatre); *To Kill A Mockingbird* (West End).

Judith Volk
Deputy Stage Manager

Judith trained at the Royal Welsh College of Music and Drama.

Previous work includes numerous productions with Creation Theatre at various locations around Oxford, the London Library and online digital work, most recently *Much Ado About Nothing* at SOAP (co-pro with OVO, St Albans); *Elephant* (Bush Theatre); *Red Riding Hood and the Big Bad Pig* (JW3); *The Watsons, On the Other Side of the War, Our Town* and *The Seagull* (Oxford School of Drama); *Fragments* (Potential Difference Theatre – Playground Theatre and The Old Fire Station); *Road* and *Beryl* (Oldham Coliseum); *When The Long Trick's Over* (High Tide and New Wolsey Theatre); *Waiting for Lefty* (Two Lines Productions, online); *Amelie* (Hartshorn and Hook, tour); *Persuasion* (Theatre 6, tour) and several productions with the Royal Central School of Speech and Drama.

Charlotte Smith-Barker
Assistant Stage Manager

Charlotte studied English Literature and Film at Aberystwyth University and Malmö University in Sweden. Upon graduating in 2018, she completed the Association of British Theatre Technicians Bronze Award. When not working in theatre, Charlotte teaches English as a foreign language.

ASM credits include: *Aladdin* (Hackney Empire Theatre); *Brassed Off* (Aberystwyth Arts Centre); *You Bury Me* (Bristol Old Vic, Edinburgh Lyceum, Orange Tree Theatre); *One Woman Show* (Ambassadors Theatre); *Mary* (Hampstead Theatre); Cages (Riverside Studios); *Roundabout Tour* (Paines Plough); *Clybourne Park* (Park Theatre); *Soho Cinders* (Extension) (Charing Cross Theatre); *The Sweet Science of Bruising* (Wilton's Music Hall); *The Catherine Tate Show Live* (Wyndham's Theatre).

As Set Dresser: *The Friends Experience* (Amsterdam & Dublin).

As Prop Supervisor: *Götterdämmerung*, *L'Elisir D'Amore* (Longborough Festival Opera).

Matthew Carnazza
Production LX

Matthew trained at Rose Bruford College and specialised in lighting design and programming for Theatre and Dance.

Theatre credits as Lighting Designer include: *The Light House* (Leeds Playhouse/UK Tour); *Tomorrow is Already Dead* (Soho Theatre); *Cinderella* (UK Tour); *The Girl With The Tale* (Dance City); *Dance Nation* (Omnibus Theatre); *122 Love Stories* (Harrogate Theatre); *Against* (ALRA); *The Producers* (Bridewell Theatre); *The Collective* (Dance City/UK tour); *Vernon God Little* (Stratford Circus); *Our House* (Italia Conti); *Tutu Trouble* (Fairfields Halls); *JV2* (Sadler's Wells/UK tour).

Theatre credits as Associate Lighting Designer or Programmer include: *You Bury Me* (Bristol Old Vic); *Nutcracker* (Southbank Centre); *Bloom Dance Project* (International Tour); *Here* (Southwark Playhouse); *The Clothes They Stood Up In* (Nottingham Playhouse); *ALiCE* (JV H.O.M.E./UK tour); *Mikado* (UK tour); *Infinite Ways Home* (UK tour).

ORANGE TREE THEATRE

A powerhouse of independent theatre

We are a local theatre with a global reputation.

A show at the Orange Tree is close-up magic: live, entertaining, unmissable. We're an intimate theatre with the audience wrapped around the stage. We believe in celebrating what it means to be human. We believe in putting people at the centre of the stories we tell. And we believe in the power of a writer's words, an actor's voice, and an audience's imagination to transport us to other worlds and other lives.

We punch above our weight to create world-class productions of new and contemporary drama, revitalise classics and re-discoveries, and introduce children and young people to the magic of theatre.

We are deeply rooted in our local community in South West London. We work with thousands of people aged 0 to 100 in Richmond and beyond through participatory theatre, bringing generations together to build confidence, connection, and joy. Our ground-breaking Primary Shakespeare and Shakespeare Up Close projects pack the theatre with children and ignite a spark to last a lifetime.

We're a registered charity (266128). With only 180 seats and no support from Arts Council England, we rely on the generosity of our audiences and donors to raise £500,000 a year. These funds support our outstanding work on stage and in the community and invest in the next generation of talent.

Artistic Director **Tom Littler**
Executive Director **Hanna Streeter**

orangetreetheatre.co.uk

LONDON BOROUGH OF
RICHMOND UPON THAMES

E
T
T

ETT (English Touring Theatre) are a UK based international touring company currently celebrating their 30th anniversary. They stage both new and classic productions of outstanding quality, imagination, and ambition; make innovative and pioneering immersive digital experiences; work which interrogates and celebrates contemporary England, reinventing the rules, reflecting the diversity of the nation. You can find our work in your local theatre, online, at festivals, in a field, internationally and in the West End. In the last five years ETT has produced over 50 live productions and pieces of digital work, enjoyed by audiences of over 340,000; and has won the UK Theatre Awards Best Touring Production in 2014, 2015, 2016; Best New Play Revival in 2019; Excellence in Inclusivity and Best Play in 2022; and Excellence in Touring in 2023.

Major productions include a revival of *Equus* by Peter Shaffer in a co-production with Theatre Royal Stratford East, directed by award winning director Ned Bennett, which transferred to Trafalgar Studios; *Othello*, which toured internationally to the Far and Middle East; *Trailer Story* (a travelling outdoor performance programme that celebrated local creativity); immersive virtual reality experience Adult Children and XR experience *Museum of Austerity*, directed by Sacha Wares in partnership with Donmar Warehouse, National Theatre Storytelling Studio, ScanLAB Projects and Trial and Error. More recently *Cat on a Hot Tin Roof*, a co-production with Curve and Liverpool Everyman and Playhouse, directed by Anthony Almeida, the winner of the 2019 RTST Sir Peter Hall Director Award. A national tour of Tonderai Munyevu's *Mugabe, My Dad & Me*; A national tour of *The Importance of Being Earnest*, directed by 2021 RTST Sir Peter Hall Director Award winner Denzel Westley-Sanderson; *The Cherry Orchard* reimagined by Vinay Patel; *The Good Person of Szechwan* reimagined by Nina Segal and directed by Anthony Lau; and a national tour of *I, Daniel Blake*, written for stage by Dave Johns; and a national and international tour of *Macbeth*, directed by Richard Twyman.

ETT are a limited company and a registered charity, founded in 1993. We are based in London Waterloo.

Website ett.org.uk | **Email** admin@ett.org.uk
X @weareETT | **Facebook**/**Instagram** EnglishTouringTheatre | **YouTube** ETT

At the Octagon Theatre in Bolton, we believe in the transformative power of theatre and the arts. Our mission is simple: to bring people together and enrich communities through the magic of storytelling and creativity. We want you to feel heard and cherished in a community that is full of Northern wit, warmth, and grit.

Our unique, intimate, and flexible auditorium is home to productions that are bold, adventurous and popular, putting audiences in the heart of the action – kindling collective joy and unforgettable experiences.

Our engagement programmes provide creative opportunities for all ages. We believe that everyone has their own story, and that theatre is an amazing tool for sparking and building the confidence of people to tell theirs.

We strive to make the world a brighter place through artistic expression and collaborating with our communities.

Join us at the Octagon — a place where magic happens, and stories come alive.

The Octagon is led by Chief Executive **Roddy Gauld** & Artistic Director **Lotte Wakeham**.

Winner, Manchester's Leading Arts and Cultural Venue 2023. Nominated, UK Theatre of the Year 2023.

The Octagon is a registered charity, number 248833.

FUNDERS

GMCA GREATER MANCHESTER COMBINED AUTHORITY

PRINCIPAL SPONSOR

PRINCIPAL PATRON
Sue Hodgkiss, CBE DL

TESTMATCH

Kate Attwell

Author's Note

I often begin a play from a visual impulse. For *Testmatch*, I found myself – up late at night while jetlagged – watching a replay women's T20 match and was struck by how brilliantly fierce and powerful women in cricket kit look. It was not a sport I had thought about for a long time; it was something I played briefly in primary school before being promptly ushered into 'girls' sports. And yet now, here were these incredible athletes playing a blindingly fast version of the game, dressed like they were going to battle.

I wrote *Testmatch* while living in New York, and in many ways it is a response to (then) recent events – the murder of Trayvon Martin and the growth of the BLM movement. I was surprised – naively? – at much of white America's inability to reckon with the fact that their past, their history, was not accounted for and might still have an acute impact in the world today. I grew up in South Africa during the Truth and Reconciliation Commission (a restorative justice process in the 1990s following the end of Apartheid). We can (and should) debate the merits and failings of the TRC – but what struck me as a child, as the hearings were broadcast live on a daily basis — was a sense that neutrality and avoidance were not an acceptable status quo. Each day one could witness the most excruciating scenes of pain, of confrontation, and somehow, sometimes, of forgiveness: scenes of people reckoning with the darkest parts of themselves, scenes of people reopening the saddest wounds. It was brutal, and yet it was also a time of immense hope, of seeing a whole country try to stretch itself, empathetically, further than you'd imagine possible. That kind of emotional expansiveness has deeply impacted me; it taught me that feelings can be political, too. Here in England, I believe we still have work to do on that front: acknowledging the realities of our history.

With cricket, I found an opportunity to use the sport as a kind-of mirror for thinking about things that are systemic and structural, looking through the sport to the connection between various kinds of desires to own and exploit both land and feminine bodies.

It has also always felt natural to discuss cricket in the context of theatre, both sport and theatre are – for me – constructs – and when theatre is overtly theatrical, when it acknowledges its own 'constructedness' that is when it allows us to perhaps make visible the constructs that hold power over our world – gender, race, capitalism, language, to name a handful. The rules. Who is playing by the rules, and who isn't? Who is told they have to play by the rules, and who is told that the rules don't even apply to them? And, more importantly, what rules do we need to dismantle? And how quickly can we do it?

Kate Attwell, April 2024

Acknowledgements

There are so many folks I must thank for their contributions
to the life of this play: Diane and the team here in London.
Pam, Andy and Joy at A.C.T. in San Francisco who gave me
an artistic home and took a leap in believing in me, and also
believing that their American audiences would come to a play
ostensibly about cricket. And to every actor who has helped
develop it through multiple workshops and readings in various
cities – I am so grateful for your artistry and time.

6

Characters

INDIA 1
INDIA 2
INDIA 3
ENGLAND 1
ENGLAND 2
ENGLAND 3

ONE, *male member of the EIC Cricket Club in India*
TWO, *male member of the EIC Cricket Club in India*
DAANYA, *a villager*
MESSENGER, *a messenger*
ABHI, *One's housekeeper*
MEMSAHIB, *the memsahib, wife of One*

Notes on Text

Generally, lines should run at speed.

A (—) is a thought unfinished by the speaker.

Line breaks are intentional.

A line that ends without punctuation should be followed swiftly
by the next, almost – thought not actually – cut off. Words in
[brackets] may or may not be spoken by the actor, your choice.
Unorthodox capitalisations deliver emphasis, or noteworthiness,
as do underlines.

The text is punctuated to the musicality of the dialogue, not
grammatical correctness.

Please make every effort to produce this play sustainably.

*This text went to press before the end of rehearsals and so may
differ slightly from the play as performed.*

PART ONE

A players' lounge, a tea room, or a viewing area on the side of the field.

LOUD music.

Women's World Cup, England vs. India.

The present.

ENG 1, 2, 3.

INDIA 1, 2, 3.

All wear their One Day kit.

Some of the players' bags or belongings may be dotted about.

When players are not directly involved in dialogue, they should return to warm-up activities, make more tea, assess the rain, etc.

The door to the room bursts open and the players burst in, dripping wet and mad:

INDIA 1. This bloody country!

INDIA 2. And its bloody rain!

ENG 1. What the hell was that!

ENG 2. Couldn't see a shitting thing could I

ENG 1. That's not an excuse you play till the <u>last ball</u>,
  You don't give them a chance
  Not a bloody chance, we own them, we stay on it!
  You think you're getting paid to drop a catch?

ENG 2. Oh stop it

INDIA 2. Knew this would happen

ENG 1. What the hell

ENG 2. Bloody tits and wank is what

  ENG 3 *entering* —

INDIA 1. Well what'd he say?

ENG 3. Told me it was likely off – done and dusted

INDIA 1. What?!

ENG 3. Yeah

INDIA 1. Seriously?

ENG 3. That's what he's saying

INDIA 1. But they haven't officially called it?

ENG 3. Not yet
But they don't think it's going to stop raining all day

INDIA 2. Who said?

ENG 3. Our coach

INDIA 1. He's not the weather man

ENG 3. Well he's checked the weather

INDIA 1. Still. It's not his call

INDIA 2. I think it's off

INDIA 3. Don't jinx it

INDIA 2. Like I can influence this terrible weather?
Rain rain rain —
No way we're going to go out there again.
There's no way!

INDIA 1. Hey, stay positive – we're doing so well out there!
She just scored sixteen off the last over!

INDIA 3. I know! That was brilliant! And that last one way into
the stands —

INDIA 2. I'm only trying to be ready for the possibility that we
won't finish this match —

INDIA 1. You always do this

INDIA 2. Do what? What do I do?

INDIA 1. Moody moody pessimism

ENG 3. She's probably right

INDIA 1. Come on, you just don't want us to keep playing
      because we're doing so well —

ENG 3. No, it's not that —

INDIA 1. Are you sure?

INDIA 3. Look there's nothing anyone can do
      We'll know soon enough

INDIA 2. Remember when we played here last May?

INDIA 3. The test?

INDIA 2. Pouring rain

INDIA 3. Yes – okay, day one, it rains for a few hours,
      Then the sun came out like nothing happened.

INDIA 1. You see, hey, it could be fine!

INDIA 3. Stayed sunny the next three days too

INDIA 1. Exactly. Good. Good point.

ENG 3. Anyway, no use guessing.
      It'll only drive you crazy, drives me crazy.
      Cup of tea?

INDIA 1. Yes. Thanks.

ENG 3. Milk?

INDIA 1. Yes.

ENG 3. Cup of tea?

INDIA 3. Thank you.

ENG 3. Cup of tea?

INDIA 2. No thanks.

ENG 3. There you go.

INDIA 1. Thanks.

ENG 3. Cup of tea?

ENG 1. No thanks.

ENG 3. What're you doing?

ENG 1. Just looking at it.

They watch the rain.

ENG 3. Bollocks

INDIA 1. Shit.

She watches the rain.

Shit shit shit.

ENG 1. Yeah.

INDIA 3. It's not that bad, we could play

ENG 1. I agree

INDIA 2. You guys it's pouring!

ENG 2. Nah, it's just

INDIA 3. It always comes and goes

ENG 2. Exactly
    Comes and goes

INDIA 2. No it's here to stay, moved in, taken over, wet wet wet

INDIA 1. We get through the entire tournament,
    For weeks, no rain at all —
    And the highlight of our season —
    Our biggest match and we're out there doing bloody
    brilliantly
    It rains out!

ENG 2. What do you mean?

INDIA 1. What?

ENG 2. Highlight, what do you mean?

INDIA 1. Hey? Are you joking?

ENG 2. No

INDIA 1. We're playing against England, in England.
    And we want to win this year for sure —

INDIA 3. It's a massive match

ENG 2. Yeah but —
　　You're saying highlight, isn't that a bit premature?

ENG 1. Yeah you're not tapped to win

INDIA 1. Uh,
　　Yes we are
　　And we will.

ENG 3. To be fair —

ENG 1. You barely qualified

ENG 2. Exacto!
　　You're not even ranked that high!

INDIA 3. What? That's not true!
　　Anyway, you qualified automatically as hosts so don't even —

INDIA 1. The only reason we came in with less points
　　Is because we had to abandon that one match against
　　Pakistan
　　And you know it.

INDIA 3. We have an advantage over you – we beat —

ENG 1. Australia earlier this year?

INDIA 3. Yes

ENG 1. They're not that good

INDIA 3. Are you joking?

INDIA 1. Of course they are!

ENG 1. It's the worst team they've fielded in years,
　　Everyone knows it.

INDIA 1. That's insane

ENG 3. Well you beat them in a test, this is the World Cup.
　　This is one-dayers.
　　It's a different, you know, mindset.

INDIA 1. Well our minds are set to win.

ENG 3. This is the first time the World Cup has been held in
　　England in years.
　　We're not going down without a fight, sorry mate.

ENG 1. We're not going down at all.

INDIA 3. We'll see

INDIA 2. If we even finish playing —

INDIA 1. I hate this rain

ENG 1. We <u>have</u> to play today.

INDIA 3. I'm sure we will. I can feel it.

INDIA 2. When's the reserve day, are we rescheduling?

ENG 1. I don't want to reschedule.
I want to get it done today.
Okay?

ENG 3. Fingers crossed mate

ENG 2. Wait, we're rescheduling?

ENG 1. No, we're not. Not yet

ENG 2. You lot are killing me with all this weather talk.
There's nothing we can do about rain,
Just got to see what happens.
Fucking sucks, fucking stupid, fucking shite, but there's
nothing we can do about it!
So stop jabbering like a bunch of old grannies!

ENG 1. Piss off if you're going to be a dickhead

ENG 2. I am not being a dickhead

ENG 3. You're being quite dicky mate

ENG 2. I am not!

ENG 3. You are a bit

ENG 2. I'm not! I just

ENG 3. What?

ENG 2. I'm in a mood

INDIA 1. No kidding

ENG 2. I got a text from that fucking prick.
This morning.

ENG 3. Not <u>him</u> again! What does he want?

ENG 2. He said, better <u>pray for rain</u>, wink face.
     And now, here it is.

ENG 3. That is dicky

INDIA 1. True though

ENG 2. I hate him being right.

INDIA 3. Who's that, that England men's player you broke up
     with?

ENG 2. I am not ready to discuss it in public, thank you.

INDIA 3. There's no one here

ENG 3. She's having therapy

INDIA 3. He isn't the one who —

ENG 2. I said I —

INDIA 3. Okay whatever —I don't care that much,
     What about you, how's your American tennis player, then?

ENG 1. Yeah, he's nice, thanks, yeah.

INDIA 3. It must be hard.

ENG 1. What's hard?

ENG 2. I'll tell you what's <u>hard</u>

INDIA 2. Really?

ENG 2. Why not?

INDIA 2. That's not even an actual joke

INDIA 3. The distance. I couldn't do it. I need my man to be
     right here beside me.

ENG 2. Yeah, me too

ENG 1. It's alright.

INDIA 3. I want to be able to come home, look him right in the
     face,
     Unload the day, put my feet up with a beer,
     Unpack the latest match detail by detail
     Or shout at the TV together

ENG 3. He's a real darling your American

ENG 1. Yeah he is

INDIA 1. What's his ranking these days?

ENG 1. World no. twenty-one.

INDIA 2. Not quite Djokovic, is it

INDIA 3. Yeah but come on it's very good
Does he get all this?

ENG 1. All what?

INDIA 3. Like cricket, does he get it?

ENG 1. Oh right.
Yeah no.
No he doesn't.

INDIA 3. What? Not at all?

ENG 1. No

INDIA 3. So what on earth do you talk about?
I can only date cricketers.
Maybe someone who was a massive fan —
I don't know what I would say to anyone else,
Like, hello, do you like, uh —

ENG 1. Well, I explained it to him.
And it's basically stuck.
I said:
It's like baseball, with only two bases, and you can't strike
out, because you have to defend three sticks that are stuck in
the ground. If they get hit, you're out. Four points if you hit
it to the edge six points if it hits the edge no bounce one point
for each time you run to the sticks.

INDIA 3. What!

INDIA 2. That's ridiculous

ENG 1. It's close enough

INDIA 2. Is he here today?

ENG 1. No.

INDIA 2. Interesting

ENG 1. Is it

INDIA 2. You tell me.

INDIA 3. Anyway it's not like baseball 'cause we don't make
money like baseballers do

INDIA 1. Baseballers?

INDIA 3. Whatever you call them

ENG 3. Good point

INDIA 3. So what does he think of it?

ENG 1. He says it's like Quidditch

ENG 3. Bless him

INDIA 3. Like what?

ENG 3. Come on, you know

INDIA 1. Like that game from *Harry Potter*.
With the broomsticks.
The kids fly broomsticks.

INDIA 3. Oh right. I had a Tamil version of *Bedknobs and
Broomsticks*

INDIA 2. *Bedknobs and Broomsticks*?

INDIA 3. She flies broomsticks

INDIA 1. What?

INDIA 3. You said broomsticks!

INDIA 1. Yes

INDIA 3. It's a movie, I loved it, with Angela Lansbury

ENG 3. Oh yeah me too!

INDIA 3. And they fly a bed to an island of cartoon animals to
play football

ENG 3. You had a what version?

INDIA 3. Tamil

ENG 3. Translated?

INDIA 3. Dubbed

ENG 3. Oh right

INDIA 1. Beds and what?

INDIA 3. And they use magic to defeat the Nazis!

INDIA 1. Of course they do, England loves defeating the Nazis!

INDIA 2. Proudest moment, covers over everything else

ENG 3. Well that was a good bit of English history
So it's the best story to tell.
You know.

INDIA 1. Beating the Nazis?

ENG 3. Yeah

INDIA 1. Well okay but —

ENG 3. We beat the Nazis, but we didn't fuck up with that war,
Like America did,
They could have come out of that war heroes too,
But they had to go and put that bomb on the Japanese,
Looking like major arseholes for the next hundred years

INDIA 2. Okay, wow, we'll need to break down a lot of that —

INDIA 1. I think someone else might have looked like a major
arsehole if the truth was ever really told

INDIA 2. You know who
[Mr Churchill]

ENG 3. What?

INDIA 2. It's funny the parts of your history you choose to
remember, and then the other parts
you just sort of sweep away in the cupboard – never talk about
it, won't mention it, never tell another version of the story —

INDIA 1. Yeah, maybe since it was Indian rice and goods taken
to fuel the war, we should also get a little of the Nazi-beating
credit

INDIA 3. Cultural amnesia

INDIA 2. Is that what we're calling it?

INDIA 3. Apparently

ENG 2. He really can just <u>sod</u> <u>off</u>.

INDIA 3. What?

ENG 2. That tosser I dated

ENG 3. I think that means she's ready to talk about it

INDIA 1. Oh we're back to that

INDIA 2. And I'm out

ENG 2. The thing about him is this:
    He's a <u>cricket</u> boy

INDIA 3. And?

ENG 2. They're so uppity

INDIA 3. No,
    They're gentlemen!

ENG 2. Well I'm done with them.

ENG 1. Believe that when I see it.

ENG 2. What I will say, is:
    The thing about cricket boys, versus rugby boys, is this:
    Rugby boys get off that field,
    They've been scrumming around,
    and they just wanna fuck fuck fuck
    Just fuck fuck fuck because they got all that testosterone up
    inside them.
    And they're like bricks those boys. They're like tanks.
    <u>Tanks</u>
    That have been at <u>war</u>.
    And that's the reason why you should date rugby boys.
    Cricket boys, on the other hand, have not been at war,
    They will not give a fuck about fucking.
    They will want to talk. And talk and talk. About the game.
    Rugby is all these tank men at war,

Smashing at each other,
Rubbing their willys accidentally on each other,
And so then you fuck them,
And then they're like puppies.
And that's really nice.

INDIA 1. This is why I hate playing one-day matches in
England

INDIA 2. Because you got to listen to her?

ENG 2. Oh go on back to the dressing rooms then!

INDIA 1. We're rained out in the middle of the game

ENG 3. It's not like it was less likely to rain in a four-day match

INDIA 1. It is

ENG 3. That makes no sense

INDIA 1. It does

ENG 3. How?

INDIA 1. Okay look, if you've got four days and anytime
during those four days, you could have rain versus if you've
got one day, what you've got is you've got a higher chance
of it raining in the four days than the one day, but a higher
chance of it raining a hundred per cent of the one day, than
a hundred per cent of the four days.

ENG 3. What

INDIA 1. Yes

ENG 1. That sort of makes sense to me actually

INDIA 1. Just think about it!

INDIA 2. It is miserable weather.

INDIA 3. I would need a, what do you call it like a, sun lamp!

INDIA 2. You would.
It's bleak

INDIA 1. It makes the whole of Western history make sense,
this weather!

If I had to live in this, I'd get off this island as fast as I
possibly could,
And take over whatever land I came across, because anything
would be better
You know, can't you just see them like, 'We Need to Escape
this Island!'

INDIA 2 (*English accent*). We must escape this island!

INDIA 1. I can't stand the mizzle!

INDIA 2. I can't stand the grey!
    Don't you find it bloody <u>awful</u> bollocks here
    wouldn't it be better should we aboard some fairer clime!

INDIA 1. Indeed what a marvelous suggestion
    William Todd Harris Jones
    Henry the Fourth of Buckinghamglossshire

INDIA 2. Of village on the Wold-on-Sea

INDIA 1. I say I might catch a suntan I say!

INDIA 2. Sun<u>tan</u>, let's get <u>burnt</u>!

ENG 2. Alright alright alright

INDIA 2. I'm so terribly cold! I'm so terribly bored!

INDIA 1. Please please please let us land our ships!
    You don't know the horrors we've come from – the rain!

INDIA 3. The food!

INDIA 1. We must escape the island!

ENG 3. I'd believe it!

ENG 1. Look don't you bitch about it, every time I been to India
    it has rained,
    like it has bloody poured the fuck down, like fucking buckets
    pouring down

INDIA 1. In India, we don't play during the rainy season,
    Here, there's not much choice.

ENG 1. It'll stop raining, it has to.
    I'm going to check.

ENG 1 *exits*.

ENG 2. The <u>other thing</u> about rugby boys —

INDIA 2. Oh my god.

ENG 2. And this might be controversial to say —
   The other thing about rugby boys is that they're well, nicer,
   like, generally.
   Because they're playing a real team sport there,
   Like, unlike cricket boys – you can't be fixing matches, in
   rugby.
   Like, if one player got bribed to fix the outcome of a rugby
   game, it wouldn't work.
   You'd have to convince the whole team.
   And that's a lot harder.

INDIA 3. What?

ENG 2. So their whole mindset is just a different, like, mindset.

INDIA 3. That's ridiculous,
   Cricket is a team sport

ENG 2. Yeah but not really

ENG 3. Oh, thanks

ENG 2. No like: we're a team and all that
   But moment to moment of the game, we're all basically
   responsible for doing our own thing

INDIA 3. But I don't think that's true at all, it's a system, it's
   a form, that works, that works all together —

ENG 2. Okay, then: When you're batting, facing the bowler,
   how are you in a <u>team</u> with your <u>teammates</u>?

INDIA 3. Well I'm <u>in a team with them</u>

INDIA 2. I get what she's saying.

INDIA 3. What?!

INDIA 2. With rugby, there's a whole team out there at once,
   And with cricket we're not all running around in a pack —

INDIA 1. No, but

INDIA 2. <u>Yes</u>, <u>but but but</u>, it's more like, like a feat of
engineering, a beautifully constructed machine – Each cog
has to be working perfectly
To keep the whole thing going

INDIA 3. Yes, it's balanced, it's graceful, it's —

ENG 2. Yeah but it's not got that pack mentality!
Look, I love these girls, don't get me wrong,
Would literally die for them, literally I would,
But when I'm up there facing one of you bowling
It's just on me!

INDIA 2. But the game doesn't <u>mean</u> anything with just you up
there —
It's everything else going on at the same time,
We're all implicated, in each moment

INDIA 3. Exactly cricket is <u>strategies</u> —
And the strategies are for the whole <u>team</u>

ENG 2. Yeah but in the moment

INDIA 3. But it's not about the moment, it's about the whole
time, the whole match

INDIA 2. Exactly, no one can do it alone.
Everyone has to be there, everyone has to buy in.
If a team were a society, we'd be a democracy, cricket,
Not a —

ENG 2. War?

INDIA 2. Exactly —
Democracy, not war

ENG 2. But moment to moment, it's everyone for himself

INDIA 2. Herself

ENG 3. Yeah it doesn't matter if you do good in one moment
You have to keep doing good
And everyone else has to, too.

ENG 2. Fine fine fine you don't get it

ENG 3. Or you're fucked

ENG 2. Fine I said You Win
[Wrong though]

INDIA 3. No I think cricket is war. War has strategies,
cricket has strategies. War has winners and losers,
And attackers, and defenders, and rules.

ENG 3. War doesn't have rules.

INDIA 3. Yes it does. It has rules.

ENG 3. War?
There are no rules to war.
How would you win a war, if there were rules to the war?

INDIA 3. I —
Same way you win a game: being the best at the rules.

ENG 3. That is not how I would fucking win a war.
I'd go outside of the rules

INDIA 3. See, that's why I like cricket.
Cricket is not a blood sport.
Cricket is measured. It's ordered. It's —

INDIA 1. I think that's the problem with it.

INDIA 3. What do you mean problem?

INDIA 1. There's a lot buried, hiding, under that order.
It's violent, cricket, it's dangerous

INDIA 3. It's not —

INDIA 1. There's a lot buried, hiding, under that order.
That's the problem with cricket.
Cricket is like diplomacy.

INDIA 2. Ha, that's good!

INDIA 1. Evil in a suit and a tie and a handshake

INDIA 3. But you love cricket!

ENG 1 *returns*.

INDIA 1. Well? Have they made the call?

ENG 1. No, nothing yet.

ENG 2. You know, the <u>other</u> thing about cricket boys

INDIA 1. Can you talk about <u>anything</u> else?

ENG 3. It's a recent obsession.
    Since she was dumped by the men's captain

ENG 2. He did not dump me

ENG 3. Sorry – that's right – the press dumped her for him –
    Posted a bunch of pics of him out with some bloody stripper

ENG 2. She was not a <u>stripper</u>
    Those were just her clothes!
    Anyway, you shouldn't read that shite

ENG 3. I don't read it! You can't help seeing it, though, can you.
    Why you defending her anyway?

ENG 2. I'm not!
    Just she can wear whatever the fuck she wants,
    It's not my problem

ENG 3. Well, he was a narcissist wanker —

INDIA 3. You <u>are</u> finished with him, right?

ENG 2. Yeah, why, what d'you mean?

INDIA 3. I thought I read something somewhere that you were
    taking him back.

ENG 2. What?
    Where'd you read that?

INDIA 3. Well actually I didn't read it, but I was with my
    auntie, and she said that it said that you said that you were
    still seeing him.

ENG 2. Bloody hell: <u>no</u>.
    Here's what I said:
    I said to him, into his face: he lied and he lied and lied and
    lied
    And then I said, 'I'll see you around'

But meaning, piss off you arsehole,
Not like, come by my house tomorrow.
Because I will see him around!
I can't avoid him

INDIA 3. So what did happen?

INDIA 1. Stop encouraging her —

INDIA 3. But I wanna know! It's good gossip,
You just found out and ended it?

ENG 2. No he did.

INDIA 3. Oh that's bad

ENG 2. Yeah it was bad

INDIA 3. Was it in a text?

ENG 2. What?

INDIA 2. Men are terrible

ENG 2. No it was in person. But it was a little too little a little
too late,
You know what I mean.

INDIA 2. Yeah

INDIA 3. I do

INDIA 1. I don't think that's how that saying goes

ENG 2. What saying?

INDIA 1. What you just said: A little too little a little too late.

ENG 2. No

INDIA 1. Yes no

ENG 2. How's it go then?

INDIA 1. I think it's: a little too little too late.

ENG 2. What?

INDIA 3. You said the same thing.

INDIA 2. A little too little —

INDIA 1. No, she said,
   a little too little a little too late.

INDIA 3. Yeah… so

INDIA 1. And I think it's:
   A little too little, too late.

INDIA 3. Same thing, no?

INDIA 2. Is it?

INDIA 1. No

ENG 2. I'm pretty sure it's:
   A little too little, a little too late

INDIA 1. I don't think so

ENG 2. Because it's doing a little too little a little too late

INDIA 1. No it's doing:
   A little too little, <u>Too Late</u>

ENG 2. So it's any amount of late then?

INDIA 2. Right like, a year later, but it's still too little, to make
   up for whatever you did?

ENG 2. Or five years

INDIA 2. But still, it's not enough

INDIA 3. Oh I see
   So it means —

ENG 2. But I think it's better if it's too little and also a little
   <u>too late</u> —
   Like, you <u>only barely</u> missed it.

INDIA 1. No 'cause it's too little <u>no matter</u>

ENG 2. No this is better 'cause it's like: you missed it by a
   second

INDIA 1. But it's more, you know, meaningful, if it <u>could be</u>
   like a whole year

INDIA 2. Or a hundred years

INDIA 1. The whole of history! But you still did nothing

INDIA 2. Ha, exactly

ENG 2. What?

ENG 3. Isn't it just too little too late?

> ENG 1 *suddenly smashes her bat hard onto the ground, repeatedly, yelling.*
>
> *All jump and stare.*

ENG 1. AHH What the fuck
Shut the fuck up!
Stop this stupid rain fuck!

ENG 3. Whoa, what on earth!

ENG 1. Fucking stop fucking raining

ENG 3. Oy, mate!

ENG 2. What the hell

ENG 1. I want to play

ENG 3. Mate if we can't finish play today —

ENG 1. No we have to.

ENG 3. Yeah, we want to but —

ENG 1. I'm ready, we're all ready,
Let's just go out there —
Does anyone else want to go out there with me and just play —

ENG 3. Slow down, gimme the bat

ENG 1. Okay.
Shit.

ENG 3. Yeah you broke that shit

ENG 1. It's fine

ENG 3. You got another one?

ENG 1. In the dressing room.

ENG 3. Okay.
Shall we go get it?

ENG 1. It's fine. I don't need it. I'm fine.

ENG 3. Okay.

ENG 1. I'm fine

ENG 3. Of course

ENG 1. We just really have to keep playing today,
    That's all.
    Why don't you all just leave me alone.

INDIA 1. Hey, no one was even talking to you

INDIA 3. We were having a linguistic debate!

ENG 2. Mate, seriously, what's going on?

ENG 1. I'm stressed out —
    Aren't you?

ENG 3. Let's go for a walk

INDIA 1. Of course we are, we were doing great out there,
    owning the game,
    Already it's a brilliant score for you to chase —
    But I'm not stomping and smashing and throwing shit around
    am I?

ENG 1. Well good for you

INDIA 1. Come on princess, calm down

ENG 2. Oy, that's not on

INDIA 1. It's a joke!

INDIA 2. Sort of

ENG 2. Why don't you just shut the

INDIA 1. Don't you talk to me like that

ENG 2. I'll talk however I want you

ENG 3. You know what, you know what:
    Conflict diffusion over here!
    Come on, you, let's go get your other bat.
    We should all get out of here anyway.
    Come.

ENG 1 *considers*.

ENG 1. Yeah okay.

Pause.

ENG 2. I'm coming too.

ENG 1, 2 *and* 3 *exit.*

INDIA 1. Oh my god, what was that

INDIA 3. I know!

INDIA 2. She actually broke the bat

INDIA 3. Who does that?
What is up with her?

INDIA 1. Crazy actually crazy

INDIA 3. I don't think that's how a captain should behave.
Not here, in the open

INDIA 1. Not anywhere

INDIA 3. Not anywhere! That's not how a cricketer should act
That's not in line with the values of the game

INDIA 1. She can be a little, I don't know, uptight sometimes
but that was —
That was actually crazy

INDIA 3. You think there's something going on with her?

INDIA 1. What do you mean

INDIA 2. Like what?

INDIA 3. Like maybe it's the time of the month you know or

INDIA 2. Come on, don't go low

INDIA 3. What's wrong with that! It could be!

INDIA 1. Oh come on, you just fancy her – defending her!

INDIA 2. Oh shush,
She's not my type.

INDIA 1. Are you sure about that?

INDIA 2. Look, that's not it!

INDIA 1. Well maybe she's being weird because you, you two,
      you know —?
      After that match in April

INDIA 2. Hey. I told you not to —

INDIA 1. Maybe that's making her act like this —

INDIA 3. What!

INDIA 2. No I told you not to say —

INDIA 3. Are you serious though?

INDIA 2. No, just leave it —

INDIA 3. I thought she has a boyfriend!

INDIA 2. Lots of people have boyfriends

INDIA 1. Ha

INDIA 2. Look at her now:
      Stop looking so shocked

INDIA 3. I'm not!
      I'm still getting used to it, with you being a lesbian, and all

INDIA 1. I still can't believe you didn't realise

INDIA 3. I'm basically from the middle of nowhere!
      There aren't so many lesbians out there

INDIA 2. Yes there are
      Believe me.
      Anyway,
      We've got more important things to think about —
      It's the World Cup!

INDIA 1. You're right

INDIA 3. So do they all know about you being a lesbian or
      something?

INDIA 2. Just drop it.

INDIA 3. They might not care

INDIA 2. It's not that I care if <u>they'd care</u>

INDIA 3. They might have some helpful advice and tips for lesbians

INDIA 2. I think I'm good, thanks.

INDIA 3. They've got a lot of lesbians on their football teams.

INDIA 2. Stop saying lesbians!
You know how much they love talking to the press, posting everything

INDIA 3. Ah that's true

INDIA 2. It'd be the death of my poor mother

INDIA 1. My god, can you imagine?

INDIA 2. Poor woman
Newspaper opens:
Mother, grandmother, entire family all dead!

INDIA 3. Ha, I can just see it!

INDIA 2. You know?

INDIA 1. They might not, though.
You never know.

INDIA 2. I do know

INDIA 1. Historically we are very queer.

INDIA 2. Queer, ha?

INDIA 1. Sure.

INDIA 3. I used to say I was a boy when I started cricket, you know, so I could play more, and my grandmother said that was right in line with what the rest of the gods were up to, so she was fine with it

INDIA 1. Exactly! You see?
Your grandmother was right

INDIA 3. She was right on everything

INDIA 2. Of course, but you know it's not the same
  Things have changed
  Things were rewritten
  Things were taken

INDIA 1. Lost to Empire

INDIA 3. Don't you hate lying to your family though?

INDIA 2. It's not lying, it's —
  Just not the whole truth.

INDIA 3. But it's an important part

INDIA 1. Leave it alone – it's her life

INDIA 2. Listen,
  One day.

INDIA 1. Yes, one day.

INDIA 3. Okay,
  As long as you're happy.

INDIA 2. I am.

INDIA 3. Okay.

INDIA 1. Come you guys, we're going to win, I can feel it, I
  want to beat them.

INDIA 3. Me too

INDIA 1. I want to beat them, completely. Squarely.
  We're going to win.
  This could be our year.

INDIA 3. This is our year!

INDIA 1. And it's only your first call-up!
  And listen, I wasn't going to say yet, but, I want to tell you,
  if we do win this, I —

  Pause.

  I'm retiring.

INDIA 3. What?!

INDIA 1. So I need it to be bloody brilliant

INDIA 2. Retiring?

INDIA 1. Yeah

INDIA 3. What?

INDIA 1. Yes

INDIA 3. What?

INDIA 1. Yeah

INDIA 3. From cricket?

INDIA 1. No, from meteorology,
Yes from cricket!

INDIA 3. But what will you do?
What on earth will you do with yourself?

INDIA 1. I'll coach. And I've been talking to AIR about this
radio idea —
Which is also why I need to go out as a winner, okay?

INDIA 3. But no more actual playing?

INDIA 1. I can't. My knee keeps going —
Twice the past year

INDIA 2. You're serious?

INDIA 1. Yeah.

INDIA 2. That's really it?

INDIA 3. I'm in shock. I'm shocked.

INDIA 1. I know you've noticed, I'm slower every game

INDIA 3. No you're not

INDIA 1. I know you've thought it —

INDIA 3. I'm shocked I'm in shock right now.
We better not play on today, as I'm in shock.

INDIA 2. Who have you told?

INDIA 3. I've been wanting to play with you my whole life!

INDIA 1. Just you two. Just now.

INDIA 3. And coach?

INDIA 1. He knows yeah

INDIA 3. It has been an honor to play with you.

INDIA 2. She's not dying!

INDIA 1. So I'd love this:
  To win this game, fair and square and absolutely,
  To hold that moment.

INDIA 3. We can do it!
  We will make you proud

INDIA 1. Look,
  Keep it on the down low, okay

ENG 2 *and* 3 *re-enter.*

ENG 3. Alright, we've got another bat,
  She's taking a minute.
  Sorry about all that.

INDIA 1. That's okay. Where did you go?

ENG 3. Dressing room

INDIA 1. Any word on the call? Will we resume?

ENG 3. Nothing yet.

INDIA 1. Come on!

ENG 3. I know

ENG 2. You know the real thing, about cricket boys versus
  rugby boys —

INDIA 1, ENG 3 *and* INDIA 2. Shut up, No babe, Oh my god

ENG 2. What?!
  I just wanted to finish my point!

ENG 3. Go on then

ENG 2. That there's none of this bloody cheating that the men
  do!

INDIA 1. What do you mean?

ENG 2. It's what everyone in the dressing room's talking about!

INDIA 3. My god I know did you see the news yesterday —

ENG 2. That's it! That's my point!
Biggest fix in years,
What a stupid nob.

INDIA 1. Alright, I'll agree with you in this case.

ENG 2. Thank you!

INDIA 2. These guys are so crazy. I thought it was a thing of the
past.

INDIA 3. Me too

INDIA 2. I guess not

INDIA 3. But there it is, still happening, in black and white.
Only better hidden most of the time.

ENG 2. Lazy fucks. I suppose it's just how it is over there, isn't
it.

INDIA 2. What do you mean by that?

ENG 2. Oh I

ENG 3. Who wants another cup of tea?

INDIA 2. No, what did you mean?

ENG 2. I just meant, I meant,
I meant, you know

INDIA 2. Oh I know.

ENG 3. Cup of tea?

INDIA 2. No thanks.

INDIA 3. I'll take one.

ENG 3. Great!

INDIA 3. Hey, do you all remember when that South African
guy —

INDIA 1. Oh yeah the captain?

INDIA 3. Yeah, sure, him, but no I didn't even mean that guy,
but the other white guy, just kept bowling wides. 'Best in
the world' and then every other tournament, every ball was
a wide!

INDIA 2. Banned for two seasons

INDIA 3. Better have been worth the money

ENG 3. I know

INDIA 3. I could never do that.

INDIA 2. Well those gangs and bookmakers don't care about us,
do they,
Our women's matches

INDIA 1. I don't know if that's a good thing or a bad thing

INDIA 3. I can't even imagine it,
Being banned. The rules of cricket are, beautiful, to me.
They're perfect.
I started playing when I was three, with my dad.
If I got banned now —

INDIA 2. I don't know what I'd do.

INDIA 3. Could you still play in a different sport?

INDIA 2. I don't know

INDIA 3. Not that I even play a different sport:
It's been my whole life,
Learning this game,
Learning every detail,
Every possibility,
Every outcome
It's like, it really is the way my whole life is structured.
It's what controls my body,
Like, how I wake, sleep, what I eat, why I eat it and when,
I don't know what I'd be if I lost that just like, a stone... or
a fish swimming along —

INDIA 1. Well you're not going to do something like that, so
    you're not going to be a fish, okay?
    It's always a choice to do something, or not.

INDIA 2. Yes

ENG 2. Yes exactly

    ENG 1 *enters*.

INDIA 1. There she is!

ENG 1. Hey.
    What you guys talking about?

INDIA 1/ENG 2. Fixing

ENG 1. What? Why?

INDIA 1. The news from yesterday

ENG 1. Oh yeah right yeah of course.
    Well it's money isn't it.
    I mean, that's all it is.

INDIA 1. Okay, but

ENG 1. We all need money.
    Not like we're making millions, any of us

INDIA 2. The boys do though

ENG 1. Not millions

INDIA 2. Close to it

INDIA 1. Oh come on, you can't be doing badly —
    Rumour is you've got a massive deal,
    Who's your latest endorsement from?

ENG 1. It's not massive

ENG 3. Go on, tell them,
    It's a good one

ENG 1. It's not a big deal

ENG 3. It is a big deal

INDIA 2. Yeah come on!

INDIA 1. Who you modeling for?

ENG 1. Max Factor.

ENG 3. Max Factor!

INDIA 1. Max Factor?
  God, you got cosmetics.
  That's wild.
  That hardly ever happens.

ENG 2. Never, that hardly never happens
  It's amazing.

INDIA 1. Well, well well!

ENG 1. Oh go away, all of you

INDIA 1. Legs for days, rosy cheeks

INDIA 3. Played for the English national cricket and football
  teams

  (*To* INDIA 2.) Even you'd buy make-up off her!

INDIA 2. I'm going to see if I can find something to eat.

INDIA 3. No I didn't mean it like —

INDIA 2. It's fine.

  Pause.

INDIA 3. Would you get me something?

INDIA 2. Okay.

INDIA 3. Hey, what are the others doing now?

INDIA 1. Must be in the dressing room still.
  Where's the rest of your team?

ENG 1. Dressing room, and some are in that bar upstairs

INDIA 3. Should we all go to the bar?

INDIA 1. If you want.

INDIA 2. Hey, you okay, you want anything?

ENG 1. No thanks.

ENG 2. Hold on a minute

INDIA 2. What?

ENG 2. I'm coming with you

INDIA 2. Oh god.

ENG 2. What – I need food.

INDIA 2. Come along then.

ENG 2 and INDIA 2 *exit.*

Long, long pause.

INDIA 1. Still bloody raining.

ENG 1. Yeah.

INDIA 1. Still waiting to hear.

Pause.

ENG 1. Sorry I got stressed.

Pause.

INDIA 1. No I get it.
Big match.

Pause.

You know what I sometimes think?

ENG 1. What?

INDIA 1. It's like we've known each other, for years, but we have no back story

ENG 1. What do you mean

INDIA 1. We keep meeting each other at matches, year after year,
And it's sort of the same thing each time
We chat, we play, we go out there

ENG 1. That's the nature of sport I guess. A kind of déjà vu, of
    doing the same thing,
    We've played each other how many times now?

INDIA 1. I couldn't say

ENG 1. But I think you've been playing the longest of us all.

INDIA 1. I certainly have.

ENG 1. Must be taking its toll

INDIA 1. Twelve years.

ENG 1. That's —
    A long time.

INDIA 1. Yeah.

   Pause.

   So you're feeling better?

ENG 1. Yeah I'm fine.

INDIA 1. Good, good. Okay —

   I'm gonna get something to eat too.

   INDIA 1 *exits.*

   INDIA 3, ENG 1 *and* 3 *remain.*

   INDIA 3 *lies down on a bench and closes her eyes.*

   ENG 3 *and* 1, *quietly:*

ENG 3. What's up.

ENG 1. Nothing.

ENG 3. You're all jumpy, you won't talk —
    You wouldn't even talk about your new Max Factor thing —
    You love talking about that!
    What's up.

ENG 1. Nothing.

ENG 3. I know you better than this, What's up?

   Pause.

She looks over at INDIA 3 *to make sure they're not being overheard.*

ENG 1. It's —

Pause. Looks over again.

It's nothing. I wanted to play today. I'm frustrated. It's nothing.

Pause.

Also they're fucking pissing me off.

ENG 3. What, why?

ENG 1. Just are

ENG 3. Is it about WinViz?

ENG 1. What?

ENG 3. 'Cause just 'cause WinViz say they're gonna win, Doesn't mean they're gonna win.

ENG 1. Of course not!

ENG 3. We've got home advantage

ENG 1. Yeah.

ENG 3. And we've got you

ENG 1. Yeah

ENG 3. Then what?

Pause.

ENG 1. Look, don't take the piss okay?

ENG 3. Okay —

ENG 1. I'm —

ENG 3. What?

ENG 1. I was feeling, I am feeling,
    A bit, scared

ENG 3. Scared?

ENG 1. A little

ENG 3. Of what?

Pause

ENG 1. Of her.

ENG 3. Her who? The captain?

ENG 1. She's an amazing bowler

ENG 3. Oh, come on, she's just a fast bowler

ENG 1. Well
I'm a little

ENG 3. Scared

ENG 1. On edge about it. And —

She looks around in case INDIA 3 *might hear.*

You know.
She is,
She's the best.

ENG 3. Well but —
It's just, that's, it's just rankings, it doesn't mean anything

ENG 1. Best

ENG 3. But you're the best batter

ENG 1. So

ENG 3. By those same standards,
You're the best batter

ENG 1. I know

ENG 3. You've been playing for England since you were
What —

ENG 1. Still

ENG 3. Sixteen?

ENG 1. So

ENG 3. So,
You got this.

ENG 1. Yeah but, look.
    Here is a list of things I like:
    Number one: winning.

ENG 3. Okay —

ENG 1. And that's it
    That's the end of the list.

ENG 3. Well we will!

ENG 1. But if she, you know if she was to, bowl me,
    <u>If</u> she got me out, I —

ENG 3. What

ENG 1. You know I like to be in control of the game: my game

ENG 3. Yeah

ENG 1. No matter what,
    And she makes me

ENG 3. What

ENG 1. Forget it.
    I just wanna get it over and done with.

ENG 3. Well,
    Look, I get it, and I didn't want to bring this up before,
    But,
    If we don't keep playing today
    It's not necessarily a bad thing
    It's raining, you know, rain —

ENG 1. Could be on their side

ENG 3. Exactly.
    So it's possibly no bad thing:
    They're a much stronger fielding team, they're a great
    bowling unit.
    We're a much stronger team batting.
    We've got you,
    But yeah, they're a strong fielding team.
    She's a really good bowler.
    I'm just saying, it's not that I don't think we'll win, of course
    not but

But I'm not sure it would have been good for us to play
today.
You know?

Pause.

ENG 1 *considers.*

ENG 1. Okay let's drop it.

ENG 3. And don't worry about her.
    Even if we do play.

ENG 1. It's not a big deal
    It's fine

ENG 3. Good

ENG 1. Don't you dare tell anyone what I said

ENG 3. Obviously.

ENG 1. I mean it

ENG 3. Okay!

    ENG 2 *returns with a bottle of juice.*

ENG 3. What you get?

ENG 2. Some kinda mango juice.

ENG 3. Can I have a sip.

    ENG 2 *passes her the drink.*

    Jesus Christ.

ENG 2. What?

ENG 3. That is the sweetest thing I have ever tasted

ENG 2. It's good for you!

ENG 3. I don't think there's any mangoes even in there, just
    sugar

ENG 2. Then don't drink it.

ENG 3. I won't

ENG 2. Great

ENG 3. They could sell sewerage with that much sugar and call it mango juice.
Capitalist dickheads.

ENG 2. It's just a juice babe.
What were you two talking about anyway?

ENG 1. Nothing.

INDIA 1 *and* 2 *return*

INDIA 1. Okay.
There is no way we're going back on – I took a walk out there.

INDIA 3 *sits up*

The pitch is soaked.

INDIA 3. I can't believe this!
Why don't they just let us go now.

ENG 1. It's got to get called officially

ENG 2. Taking their sweet time then

INDIA 2. This is why I love playing in Australia.
Never rains there.

ENG 3. I've been rained off at least twice in Australia

INDIA 1. Yeah but when it rains in Australia, it's a real downpour,
Not this miserable shit

ENG 1. Oh shut up!

INDIA 1. God, you really are so twitchy today!

INDIA 3. I'd be nervous too if I were you.

ENG 1. What d'you mean by that?

INDIA 3. What do you mean what do I mean?

ENG 1. You fucking listening to my private conversations?

INDIA 1. What are you talking about?

ENG 1. You some kind of fucking spy?

INDIA 1. What! Don't talk to my players like that
    What do you mean some kind of spy?

ENG 1. Are you trying to throw me off?

INDIA 2. Hey, come on, that's not

INDIA 1. What?

ENG 1. Snooping, listening in to what I was saying!

INDIA 1. What <u>are</u> you talking about?

ENG 1. <u>She</u> knows!

INDIA 1. I'm sure she wasn't listening to anything, and anyway,
    what have you got to hide?

ENG 1. I don't have anything to hide! I just —

INDIA 1. Yes?

INDIA 3. Don't talk in front of me like I'm not there if you
    don't want me to hear

INDIA 1. Wait, what?

ENG 2. Okay what the fuck is going on?

INDIA 3. We're just trying to figure out what's up with your
    captain

ENG 2. What's it to you?

ENG 1. That's right, there's nothing —

INDIA 1. Why she's so tense
    So uptight
    So anxious about today —

ENG 3. It's the World Cup!

ENG 2. Exactly!

ENG 1. Look, what are you accusing me of?

INDIA 1. What?

INDIA 3. <u>Accusing</u> you?

INDIA 2. They're not accusing you of anything, let's just drop it —

Come on guys I want to go —

ENG 2. Sounds like you're fucking accusing her of something What's your problem?

INDIA 2. Come on let's just go —

ENG 3. Tea? Cup of tea?

INDIA 3. There's something dodgy going on for sure

ENG 1. Oh what you think someone's cheating or something? What a laugh!

INDIA 1. Excuse me?

INDIA 3. Cheating? I didn't say —

INDIA 1. She didn't say that —

ENG 3. Wait what?

INDIA 3. I was just accusing you of being <u>scared</u> but now —

INDIA 1. Cheating?

ENG 1. So you <u>were</u> listening in?

INDIA 1. To what?

INDIA 3. Now I do think there's something more

ENG 2. Oh come on!

INDIA 3. Is that why you've been so crazy?

ENG 2. Anyone would be cheating it'd be one of your lot!

INDIA 1. <u>Excuse me</u>?

INDIA 3. Is that what's going on? Have you been talking to bookies?

ENG 3. What!

ENG 2. Are you —

INDIA 1. You hear what she just said?
    Did you hear what she just said to us?

INDIA 2. Yeah but look at her

ENG 2. What's that supposed to mean?

INDIA 2. Didn't expect any better

ENG 2. What the

INDIA 1. You are not going to get away with that —
    I'm going to go and flag that comment right now —

ENG 2. Oh really, what are you gonna say?

INDIA 1. That you —

ENG 2. You wanna start a fight?

ENG 3. No no no one is starting a

INDIA 2. Hey, guys, let's —

INDIA 1. She already started one when she started yelling and
    smashing shit up,
    While we're all just sitting here trying to take a moment and
    wait but instead —

ENG 3. She's stressed!

INDIA 1. Aren't we all!

ENG 3. Look, go sit in your dressing room if you want to be
    like this,
    None of us need to be in here

INDIA 1. No it's freezing in there, I don't want them getting
    cold

ENG 2. Yeah better not get cold,
    Don't want us to have more of an advantage

INDIA 1. This year we're the best team in the world
    You know we're going to win today

ENG 2. You wish!

INDIA 1. No, we <u>are</u>!
  <u>Look at the score we've already made today</u>!
  Do you know how hard I've worked to be the top bloody
  female bowler <u>in the world</u>,
  better than a lot of the men

INDIA 3. Every stat says we'll win today
  This is a really, a big match for us

INDIA 1. And I have a lot riding on this too but you don't see
  me acting crazy:
  So just answer us, okay?
  You got something depending on this happening today?
  You got some personal stake in not getting rained out?

ENG 3. Sorry what —

INDIA 1. Have you?

ENG 2. You are having a laugh

ENG 3. Come on, this is crazy

INDIA 1. Is it?

ENG 2. What the fuck

ENG 1. Honestly

INDIA 1. Are you on the take?
  Just answer that.

ENG 3. What! How could you say that
  Jesus Christ

ENG 1. I don't have to answer to you
  Why would I fix the match? Huh?
  I'm a star!
  Why would I need to do that

ENG 3. This is so fucked up
  She's just stressed about the game.
  It's the World Cup!
  You all should be stressed about the game!

INDIA 1. That's not really an answer

ENG 1. <u>No, then</u>!

INDIA 3. This is our game, this is our time, if you're messing around with the outcome of the match I —

ENG 2. Your game?

INDIA 3. Yes

ENG 2. You wouldn't even —

ENG 3. Hey settle down —

ENG 2. Wouldn't even have this game if we hadn't brought it to you!

INDIA 1. You really want to talk about all the things we 'wouldn't have' if you hadn't brought them?

ENG 2. Yeah, go on then
You think you're so great
You think you know anything about anything about —

INDIA 3. Hey, don't speak to her like that, she's our captain, she's —

ENG 2. And what are you, her servant?

INDIA 1. What?

ENG 3. Look stop stop stop let's just drop this it doesn't make sense it's not worth the fight

INDIA 1. But

ENG 3. The point is I'm just saying the point is look who does the most fixing in the men's games if anyone was going to fix the match,
It'd more likely be one of your —

INDIA 2. That's not true!

ENG 3. Team than —

INDIA 2. That is just not true!

INDIA 1. If you look at the <u>facts</u>, at the <u>history</u> of it —

ENG 2. Oh you're gonna give us <u>history</u> lesson?
Fuck history —
It's dead. This is now.
This has nothing to do with history!

INDIA 1. That's the stupidest thing I've ever heard.

ENG 2. You're the stupidest thing I've ever heard, you
    bloody —

INDIA 1. That is it!

ENG 2. Fuck you!

She lunges towards INDIA 1

INDIA 2 *blocks her.*

A fight ensues between all.

Then,

ENG 2 *punches* INDIA 1 *in the face,*

She falls.

Her nose is bleeding.

Pause.

INDIA 3 *helps* INDIA 1 *get up, slowly.*

She turns back to the room.

INDIA 3. Look at this.

INDIA 3 *takes an arm from* INDIA 1.

They slowly exit.

Pause.

ENG 1. You. Go for a walk.

ENG 2. What?

ENG 1. Go. Now.

ENG 2. No

Pause.

ENG 2 *exits.*

ENG 1. Shit.
    This is going to look so bloody bad.

INDIA 2. It's going to <u>look</u> bad?

ENG 1. Yeah, it's going to look bad.

Pause.

INDIA 2 *sits down.*

ENG 3 *sits down.*

ENG 3. You okay?

ENG 1. Yeah I'm fine

ENG 3. You?

INDIA 2. Yeah

Pause.

ENG 3. Why'd you let that get so out of hand?

ENG 1. What

ENG 3. Why —

ENG 1. It's not my fault!

ENG 3. You're the captain!
Look what happened —
Why not just tell them you didn't do it?

INDIA 2. Because she did.

Pause.

ENG 3. What?

INDIA 2. Come on!
How many times does she have to freak out about not
playing today,
Not even really try to hide it,
Not deny it,
For you to realise!

Pause.

ENG 3. No, fuck off

INDIA 2. Come on, tell the truth,
What's there to lose?

ENG 3. Someone just got hurt —

INDIA 2. Tell her the truth.

ENG 3. Look here —

ENG 1. Leave it.

ENG 3. No way, you hearing this?

ENG 1. Just leave it

INDIA 2. Go on, tell her.

ENG 3. Shut up

>*Pause.*
>
>Come on
>
>*Pause.*
>
>What?
>
>*Pause*
>
>Are you serious?
>Why?
>
>*Pause.*
>
>You fixed the match?
>
>*Pause.*

INDIA 2. In a match that we were going to win anyway.
How low stakes of you.

ENG 3. You weren't going to win

INDIA 2. Yes we were.

ENG 3. The only reason you might have won,
Would have been if we had played in this rain

INDIA 2. We're the better team

ENG 3. Why would you do that?

>*Pause.*
>
>For what?
>
>*Pause.*

ENG 1. For me.

Pause.

That's it.

Pause.

It doesn't matter now anyway

ENG 3. It <u>matters</u>

ENG 1. It wasn't the match, alright, it was only a little spot.
I just said I'd throw my own innings, alright?

ENG 3. No!
You're the best on our team
You can't just throw it away
What about the rest of us?

ENG 1. We're talking about a lot of money, okay?

ENG 3. No not okay

ENG 1. A lot

ENG 3. Fuck you
I would never have done that!

ENG 1. You would never have the chance to do that!
No one would care if you missed a ball or two

ENG 3. Fuck off

ENG 1. No one would notice!

ENG 3. How much money?

INDIA 2. Why even play?

ENG 3. How much did you get?

ENG 1. I'm not going to tell you

ENG 3. I wanna know how much it's worth

ENG 1. Enough.

ENG 3. So that's it?
You've been playing this game since you were six years old.
And this is where it ends up for you?

ENG 1. Come on

ENG 3. We could've tried, we could've played

ENG 1. I wasn't even thinking about the match,
  It was my own innings.
  It had nothing to do with the whole thing.
  Just me just my innings.

ENG 3. But that is part of the whole match
  It's not just about you

  Pause.

  What were you gonna do?

ENG 1. I said I'd get bowled.

ENG 3. Why?

INDIA 2. Because she'd bowl you anyway.

  Pause.

  Right?
  She's the best in the world!
  Instead of facing that, you make a deal that means
  You can always tell yourself you did it on purpose.
  That she wasn't really better than you.
  This way, you win, no matter what.

  Pause.

  Am I right?

  Pause.

ENG 1. Actually,
  You know what?

ENG 3. What?

ENG 1. Why don't you go in on it with me.
  Next time, I mean. I bet we could get a lot together.
  We're not playing today anyway.
  But next time?
  We could both do it

ENG 3. What?
    What d'you mean – no – and —
    What are you doing saying that in front of her?

ENG 1. Oh I don't care.
    She's not gonna tell.

INDIA 2. I certainly —

ENG 1. Is she?

INDIA 2. What?

ENG 1. I said, I don't think you're gonna say anything about
    this.

INDIA 2. I'm going straight to the umpire, the coaches, you're
    stupid if you think not

ENG 1. I do think not.

INDIA 2. What?
    Why wouldn't I?
    It's illegal, for a start,
    Right in front of me —
    The press would love —

ENG 1. Then the press finds out about you, too.

    Pause.

ENG 3. What?

INDIA 2. What do you mean?

ENG 1. You know.

    Pause.

INDIA 2. You wouldn't.

ENG 1. Watch me.

INDIA 2. You can't.

ENG 3. What?

    Pause.

INDIA 2. Fine.

Pause.

I won't say anything.

ENG 1. And you?
In or out?

ENG 3. I —

ENG 1. Money makes the world go round.

ENG 3. How come you knew she was cheating?

INDIA 2. You would never think she would do that.
I would.
There's your history lesson.

ENG 1. Someone has to take advantage of any given situation.

Pause.

You know what, I'm done.
Come find me if you want to reconsider.

ENG 3. I —

ENG 1 moves to exit.

She pauses.

Turns.

ENG 1. You tell anyone about this, I'll get you benched.
You know I can.

She exits.

Pause.

Pause.

ENG 3. I'm sorry.

Pause.

I had no idea.

INDIA 2. For what.

ENG 3. Well this,
    And the fight.
    The.
    Jesus. The lot of it.
    Sorry.

INDIA 2. Yeah, well, you know what —

    Pause.

    That's just a little too little, too late.

    Pause.

    They share a small laugh.

    Pause.

    You people have some fucking baggage to figure out.

ENG 3. They didn't mean anything by it.

INDIA 2. Yes they did.

ENG 3. Fuck.

INDIA 2. Yeah.

    Pause.

    Pause.

ENG 3. What would you do?

INDIA 2. About what?

ENG 3. Well you heard her.
    What would you do?

    Pause.

INDIA 2. I —.

    A challenge to ENG 3.

    I'd take the money.

ENG 3. You would?

    INDIA 2 *shrugs.*

Yeah, that's what I'm thinking,
I mean,
If it's happening anyway,
Why not right?

Exactly the response INDIA 2 *expected.*

INDIA 2. Sure.
If it's happening anyway,
Why not.

Pause.

Change to:

PART TWO

Colonial India: aesthetically perhaps eighteenth century.
Outdoors at 'The Fort', Calcutta, India.
Green grass. (Fake.)
Bird sounds. (Fake.)
Walled in.
Maybe a 'tree' in a corner.
Maybe a backdrop.
Historical. (Fake.)

ONE *stands ready with his cricket bat.*

TWO *watches,* ABHI *bowls.*

ONE. Give me another, Abhi!

ABHI. Certainly, Sahib! Big one or small one?

ONE. Big one!

> ABHI *tosses the ball a tiny way into the air.*

> ONE *bops it with his bat.*

TWO. Ah, Well done!

ABHI. Very good, Sahib

ONE. Once more!

> Big one!

> *They do it again.*

> Good good!

TWO. Excellent!

ONE. That's enough training for today.

ABHI. Very good.

ONE. Don't want to overdo it.

ABHI. Of course not.

ONE. Another excellent day of cricket training!

ABHI. Excellent, Sahib.

ONE. Do you not think my team is the greatest team?

TWO. No question.

ABHI. If you say so.

ONE. Do you not think we, the Royal Cricket Association of
England here recreated in Bengal, as The 'Lords' Cricket
Team,
Of the East India Company
Are really quite the greatest team in all the world?

TWO. No question.

ABHI. Everything is possible, sir.

ONE. Right:
What's next?

TWO. Well, the delegation from the Sultan of Bangalore should
be arriving to begin trade negotiations today

ONE. Ah yes of course
A much needed over-land connection with our holdings at
Madras!

TWO. Yes we hope to woo them and what them and befuddle
them and gain a teensy-weensy more control over a teensy-
weensy more of their territory

ONE. Trade routes, become route routes, become our routes

TWO. And in the meantime there's your agreement —
Where's the

ABHI. Here sir.
The governor general's dispatch agreement
With the East India Company
to send you

ONE. Back home!

ABHI. Indeed.

ONE. Finally. My singular and sceptered isle.

TWO. You sign here

ONE. Good good

TWO. And here.

ONE *holds up the deed and looks at it.*

ONE. Well I say.

We really are the grandest society of merchants in the universe.

Write that down, Abhi.

ABHI. What sir.

ONE. That new tag line I invented.

ABHI. I see sir.

ONE. I want to remember it.

ABHI. Of course.

ONE. Share prices have almost doubled what with our having acquired the treasury of Bengal.
We grow, despite not turning a profit!
And let's not forget all the bonuses we've popped in there for ourselves!

TWO. Smashing.

ONE. And the King's government will never know!

ABHI. Government will never know —

ONE. No! Not that bit!

ABHI. Sorry sir

He crosses out

TWO. Marvellous

ONE. And now that's done,
I may prepare to return home.

TWO. You may.

ONE. Out of this godforsaken country.

TWO. Excellent.

ONE. I must have <u>twelve</u> new mosquito itches just this
   morning!
   Twelve!

TWO. Oh my.

ONE. I counted!

TWO. Indeed.

ONE. There's one in my toe!

TWO. Terrible!

ONE. Terrible!

ABHI. Disgusting.

ONE. And then that dreadful situation
   Outside the gates —

   A very low, low sound from outside the gates.

TWO. Ghastly.

   Pause.

ONE. I can't bear it any longer.
   Right, What's next?

TWO. Let me see —

ABHI. The cricket ruling.

TWO. Ah yes! As we await the delegation we should look at the
   ruling.

ABHI. In advance of your return to the motherland,
   You are kindly requested
   By the cricket federation of
   The Royal Association of England
   To take a look to the <u>ruling</u>

That they have laid forth
In the motherland
And make a proclamation —
Here in the company territory, in India,
<u>Finalising once and for all</u>:
The rules.

ONE. Right

ABHI. Of the game.

ONE. Right.
So that everybody may play by <u>our</u> rules

TWO. Yes

ONE. And that way we'll have more fun.

TWO. Yes.
And after that

ONE. Yes

TWO. After that
I must discuss with you —
The matter of the arm.

ONE. Ah

TWO. The <u>bowling</u> arm

ONE. Right.

TWO. Yes

ONE. Fuck

TWO. Yes

ONE. That's a real shitter.

TWO. It is.

ONE. Well —
First things first

TWO. Yes first things first
To the ruling!

ONE. Abhi!

ABHI. Yes?

ONE. Read these out so we may walk them out.

ABHI. Very good.

MEMSAHIB (*Offstage*). Dah-ling!

ONE. Not now

MEMSAHIB. Dah-ling

ONE. Not now

MEMSAHIB. Dah-ling!

　　MEMSAHIB *enters*.

ONE. Not now
　　What?

MEMSAHIB. Oh my

ONE. What is it dear?

MEMSAHIB. I didn't realise you were here too.

TWO. Good day!

MEMSAHIB. Is it though?

ONE. What is it dear?

MEMSAHIB. I Needed To Tell You About
　　A Pain

ONE. A pain?

MEMSAHIB. Well I'd rather talk to you about it in —

　　Gesturing that she doesn't want to say it in front of TWO

　　TWO *moves away*.

　　I had a pain,
　　In my

　　Glancing at TWO.

　　'Lady's pillow'

ONE. What now?

MEMSAHIB. You know in my,
Petal purse — ?
My strawberry 'tea cup'?
My kitten mouth?
My vagina!

ONE. No no no stop it I got it!

MEMSAHIB. My women's troubles are double-troubled by this
terrible pain

TWO. Ah, the monthlys —

ONE. Get to the point

MEMSAHIB. I asked Abhi to double my dose of tincture
But he he he he wouldn't —

ONE. No no no don't cry!

MEMSAHIB. If I could have eighty drops

ONE. You can have as much of the stuff as you goddamn please
Abhi!

ABHI. Yes?

ONE. Give the Memsahib double her dose of opium.

ABHI. But Sahib, the doctor —

ONE. Abhi!

ABHI. Yes sir?

ONE. Give the goddamn Memsahib as much of the goddamn
stuff as she needs

MEMSAHIB. Thank you dahling.
I told you Abhi

ABHI. But Sahib, the doctor said not to —

ONE. Enough!
Both of you!
Can't you see I have important matters to attend to!

MEMSAHIB. Now, Abhi!

    MEMSAHIB *exits*.

ABHI. Sir it's making her see things —
    Strange men who aren't there
    She speaks of
    Ships arriving on the shore
    She touches her face
    Running her hands down the lines of her face, rubbing and
    rubbing,
    Yesterday morning I found her in the cupboard
    Talking with a peacock, from the garden, she said it had
    come to tell —

ONE. Just give her as much of the stuff as it takes to calm her
    down!

ABHI. But the doctor —

ONE. Abhi! I just need her quiet!

ABHI. Okay fine. Whatever you say.
    Right away.

    ABHI *exits*.

ONE. Now where were we?
    Oh —
    Abhi!

    ABHI *re-enters*.

ABHI. Yes?

ONE. Back to the ruling.

ABHI. Of course.

TWO. Good.

ONE. Now for the rules

TWO. Yes

ONE. So we might keep <u>control</u> of the game

TWO. Yes

ONE. Right, Abhi. Ready.
>   So let's pace it out:
>   If we're standing together here,
>   You walk twelve paces that a way
>   And I walk twelve this
>
>   *They pace away from one another.*
>
>   Then there stands your wicket, your stumps, which you shall
>   defend
>
>   And here stands mine.

ONE. Right: Abhi, read —

ABHI. Ye first wicket is to be exacted by ye cast up a piece
>   of money to the sky, when ye first wicket is pitched and ye
>   popping crease cut, which must be exactly thrice foots and
>   ten inches from ye wicket

ONE. Yes!
>   Continue.

ABHI. Laws for ye Strikers —

ONE. Cross check that

TWO. Got it

ABHI. Laws for ye Strikers,
>   or those that are in
>   If ye wicket is Bowled, it's Out.

ONE. Good.

TWO. Yes.

ABHI. If he strikes, or treads down,
>   or falls himself upon ye Wicket in striking,
>   but not in overrunning,
>   it's Out.

ONE. Good.

TWO. Yes.

ABHI. A stroke or nick over or under his Batt,
>   or upon his hands,

if ye Ball be held before she touches ye ground,
though she be hugg'd to the body,
it's <u>Out</u>.

ONE. Good.

TWO. Yes.

ABHI. If in striking both his feet are over ye popping Crease
and his wicket put down, except his Batt is down within,
it's <u>Out</u>.

ONE. Good.

TWO. Yes.

ABHI. If he runs out of his ground to hinder a catch,
it's <u>Out</u>.

ONE. Good.

TWO. Yes.

MEMSAHIB (*offstage*). Abhi!

ABHI *looks at* ONE.

ONE. Oh fine yes run along

ABHI *rushes out*.

All that's down?

TWO. Indeed

ONE. Let me check
Good,
Good good

ABHI *rushes back in*.

ABHI. Sir

ONE. One moment Abhi
Popping crease… good good.

ABHI. Sir

ONE. One moment

ABHI. Sir

ONE. One moment

ABHI. Memsahib would like me to tell you

ONE. Abhi!

ABHI. But

ONE. What is it?

ABHI. Memsahib said I must tell you:
    She's out of mangoes.

ONE. She's out of <u>man</u>goes?

ABHI. Yes.

ONE. Well get her another mango, Abhi

ABHI. <u>We</u> are out of mangoes, sir.

ONE. No we're <u>not</u>

ABHI. Yes indeed.

ONE. No!

ABHI. Yes.

ONE. This is <u>India</u>,
    We're not out of <u>mangoes</u>

ABHI. Out of mangoes, sir.

ONE. But, how.

TWO. Well.

ONE. Well get her a a a a –
    Get her a Pineapple

ABHI. A what?

TWO. No, that's the Americas.

ONE. Ah right.
    Well, what about a a a —
    Lychee?

ABHI. Gone, sir.

ONE. Gone?

ABHI. Unfortunately.

ONE. Well what about a —

>   *Looks to* TWO *for a suggestion.*

TWO. A a a a

ONE. Papaya. What about a <u>Papaya</u>?

ABHI. We're out of papayas, sir.

ONE, Well give her a biscuit and tell her to shut up!

ABHI. Okay perfect.

>   *Exits.*

ONE. Abhi!

>   ABHI *re-enters.*

ABHI. Yes sir?

>   *Pause.*

ONE. No mangoes?

ABHI. No, sir.

ONE. None Anywhere?

>   *Pause.*

ABHI. I have said, sir.

ONE. Well well well.

>   ABHI *exits.*

>   Abhi!

>   ABHI *re-enters.*

ABHI. Yes?

ONE. Any word on the arrival of the delegation from
Bangalore?
These trade routes won't take care of themselves.
They should be near by now, no?

ABHI. No one's heard anything.

ONE. No one's heard?

Pause. They look up at the sun.

It beats down hot.

A low, low sound from outside the gates.

ABHI. Sir

ONE. Yes Abhi

ABHI. The people outside

ONE. What people

ABHI. The people outside —
Sir what should I —

Pause.

ONE. Well?

Pause.

ABHI. I see.

ABHI exits.

ONE. Right, where were we?

TWO. Well, we have to discuss the matter of the bowling arm.
And the women.

ONE. The women who are saying they invented the arm.

TWO. Exactly.

ONE. Right.

TWO. Those women.

ONE. Abhi!

ABHI enters.

ABHI. Yes?

ONE. Bring me the letter that arrived from those terrible
women.

ABHI produces the letter, already with him.

ABHI. Here sir, the letter from the terrible women.

ONE. Read it.

ABHI *opens the letter.*

ABHI. The note from your colleagues in England reads:
Please find enclosed the letter which we hope you, in your
remote position in India, may nevertheless provide some
council on —
And then – ah – she begins:
To The Honorable Sir —

ONE. Yes yes, skip to the good bits

ABHI. Yes sir. Um.
Here
'We are thus informing you that 'twas <u>us</u> who came up with
the overarm bowling technique
As opposed to the way 'twas thrown in the older years —
With that underhand lobbing of the ball
And we thus came up with the new method of overarm
bowling
On account of our
Skirts.
The ball getting lost and enwrapped in our voluminous skirts,
Or just the plain skirts of the peasant maids
And'
Sir,
There's a diagram here demonstrating very clearly the way in
which the overarm
Does <u>indeed</u> avoid the ball becoming enwrapped in her skirt
– you can see:

Shows diagram in letter.

ONE. Skip along, Abhi. What else?

ABHI. Then she goes on
The history of it all
And then, ah, it says:
'The new technique was made popular by these peasant
maids,
And was passed on to the Duchess of Derby
Who is willing to testify

That it was their invention
And she did use it <u>earlier than you</u>
When bowling at her brother
The ball becoming tangled in her voluminous skirts
And her maids suggested the technique'

ONE. But what's the <u>matter</u>?

TWO. Give me that.

He takes the letter. Reads.

Well. My.
They're asking for a formal recognition
Not only for the invention of the current bowling technique
In writing upon a plaque in a park,
But for a portion of all club fees, dues and memberships,
To be put toward funding their women's league and games,
And finally,
For <u>their</u> league to be recognised alongside ours.
As we write up this rule book.

ONE. My.

ABHI. Sir.

ONE. I mean
I can't
We
Can't
Yes?

TWO. I mean

ONE. No

TWO. <u>No</u>

ONE. <u>However</u>

Pause.

TWO. Yes?

ONE. They are
Well.

A mumble.

TWO. What?

ONE. They are right.

TWO. What?!

ONE. They are in fact, correct, yes

TWO. How?

ONE. Well

TWO. How are they?

ONE. Well

TWO. How?
    How are they how?

ONE. I know

TWO. What will we do?

ONE. I'm thinking

TWO. We can't possibly

ONE. I'm <u>thinking</u>

TWO. Can't <u>possibly</u>
    Let them have,
    All they're asking here.
    Can't let them <u>play</u> in the <u>league.</u>

ONE. No

TWO. Can't <u>formally</u> acknowledge that a group
    Of of of of

ONE. Maids

TWO. <u>Maids</u>
    Were responsible for the greatest
    The <u>greatest</u> advancement to the <u>game</u>
    In in in

ONE. I know

TWO. So then?

ONE. Ah ha! We simply won't talk about it.

TWO. What?

ONE. That's right

TWO. Right?

ONE. We won't talk about it.

TWO. We won't mention it

ONE. Never tell their version of the story.

TWO. Really no <u>need</u> to, come to think of it

ONE. Delete it from the records.

TWO. Gone

ONE. The more practical problem here

TWO. Yes

ONE. As I see it

TWO. Yes

ONE. The practical problem
    Is that we are now
    As we play, using this technique,
    We are now quite <u>literally</u>
    Throwing like girls.
    And so whether we agree to this request or not
    The answer being, of course, <u>not</u>

    They laugh.

    The problem nevertheless remains that in reality
    We are throwing like girls.
    So.

TWO. So.

    Pause.

    <u>But</u>.

ONE. But?

TWO. It <u>is</u> a better throwing technique, is it not?

ONE. No question.

TWO. Well then we simply must

ONE. I like where you're going with this

TWO. Ignore the letter

ONE. Never received it

TWO. Lost in the post

ONE. And then you and I
     Right here right now
     On the ground
     We swear

TWO. Swear, yes

ONE. Never again to speak of this.
     Nor tell anyone else the truth.
     Of this feminine invention of the overarm bowling.
     We make a pact. Never a word.
     Right here.
     Right now.

     A challenge. TWO *considers, accepts.*

TWO. Yes.

     A pact.

     Or

ONE. Or?

TWO. Or
     We pay them.

ONE. Ah yes.

TWO. Send these —
     Peasant maids —
     A nice little sum,
     They zip it

ONE. And that'll be that.

TWO. Brilliant.
     Abhi, write up a note of payment as such and such.

ABHI. Right away.

ONE. Do you see what we did there?

ABHI. Of course.

TWO. You learn so much from us, don't you!

ABHI. Certainly, a cunning way to solve the terrible problem.

ONE. Thank god that's cleared up.
Cup of tea?

ONE and TWO *exit.*

Pause. Blank stage.

A scuffling behind the walls.

At the top of the wall

A foot appears, a leg —

DAANYA *hoists herself over the wall and jumps down, dusts herself off and looks around.*

She wears a scrappy cricket uniform.

ABHI *rushes in.*

ABHI. Hey! Stop right there!

DAANYA. Yes?

ABHI. What are you <u>doing</u>?
What <u>on earth</u> are you doing?

DAANYA. I'm here for a meeting

ABHI. What?

DAANYA. I'm here for a —

ABHI. No you're not

DAANYA. I am.

ABHI. There's no appointment in the book

DAANYA. I know.

ABHI. Then you may hop straight back over the wall.

DAANYA. No.

ABHI. How did you even get up there —

DAANYA. Climbed.
My name's Daanya. I'm from the village, just south of the
city.

She extends her hand to him.

He looks at it, baffled.

And who are you?

ABHI. Abhi.

DAANYA. Great. Now we can be friends.

ABHI. I am the number one housekeeper of this estate,
And as such,
I must ask you again,
What are you doing here?

DAANYA. I have a proposition.

ABHI. A proposition?

DAANYA. For your boss.
You like cricket?

ABHI. Uh —

DAANYA. Catch!

She tosses him a ball.

ABHI. What!

He catches.

DAANYA. Very good!

He throws it back.

And not too bad.

ABHI. I play.

DAANYA. I can tell.

ABHI. You think so?

They continue to throw the ball back and forth.

DAANYA. Yeah,
Not too bad.

ABHI. Thanks.

DAANYA. So where do you field?

ABHI. What?

DAANYA. Where do you play?

ABHI. Oh, I normally field at cover, but I'm trying to do
    something new, you see, I really want to field first or second
    slip, or even gully!
    Hey,
    That's a good arm you've got too.

DAANYA. Thanks.

ABHI. Where'd you learn that?

DAANYA. My mother.

ABHI. Really?

DAANYA. So,
    What exactly do you do. Here.

ABHI. What do you mean?

DAANYA. You do realise who you're working for, don't you?

ABHI. 'The grandest society of merchants in the universe'

DAANYA. Seriously?

ABHI. No, that was a —
    Of course not,
    Did you not catch my tone?

    He throws the ball back.

    You still haven't told me what you're doing here.

DAANYA. Why should I trust you?

ABHI. Why should I trust you?
    You go first, you're the one trespassing.

    DAANYA *catches the ball, stops throwing.*

DAANYA. Have you been outside these walls?
    Have you seen what's,

What it looks like:
The state of things out there?

A low, low humming sound from outside the gates.

ABHI. Of course I have.

DAANYA. And?

ABHI. And?

DAANYA. Yes.

Pause.

ABHI. Triage.

Pause.

Okay?

Pause.

That's what I'm doing.
One thing at a time.

DAANYA. I don't think I can agree with that.

She throws to him.

ABHI. Do you have a better plan?

DAANYA. Better than one thing at a time?

ABHI. Yes

DAANYA. Yes

ABHI. Yes, well?

DAANYA. Everything.
At the same time.

She tosses the ball back.

ABHI. That's ridiculous.

DAANYA. It's not.

ABHI. Things can't change like that.

DAANYA. They must.

ABHI. You don't see how their minds work.

DAANYA. I don't care how their minds work.

ABHI. You think they are evil.
    Don't you.

DAANYA. Don't you?

    He hands her back the ball.

ABHI. It's far worse than that.

    ONE *and* TWO *enter.*

ONE. And who the hell are you?

TWO. AHH

DAANYA. Hello

ONE. Hello?

ABHI. I'm sorry, there's —
    There's a girl here to see you.
    This girl here. To see you.
    Sir.

ONE. What?

ABHI. There's a girl here to see you, sir.

    ONE *and* TWO *exchange a glance.*

ONE. Come to see me?

ABHI. Yes, apparently so.

ONE. This is ridiculous.
    Get out of here, both of you!
    What do we need to take care of next?

TWO. Well we're done, really, until the trade delegation
    arrives —

ONE. Ah.
    Abhi?

ABHI. Yes?

ONE. Still no word from the delegation?

ABHI. No sir.

ONE. They should have arrived by now, no?

ABHI. Perhaps, sir.

ONE. Perhaps? What do you mean, perhaps?

ABHI. It's hard to tell of anything these days.
Times being what they are, things standing as they do

ONE. Hard to — ?
What?!
Honestly, Abhi.
I know —
Send a boy to Cuttack,
Have him take a horse,
See if anyone there has heard from the delegation.

ABHI. Will do.

DAANYA. I'll introduce myself since no one else is going to.
Good day, sir.

She extends her hand to ONE. *He looks at it.*

I brought you a mango.

ONE. Ah!
Abhi!

ABHI. Yes?

ONE. Give this mango to the memsahib.

ABHI *takes the mango carefully.*
He holds it and stares at it.
And stares at it.
He exits.

What're you called?

DAANYA. Daanya, sir.

ONE. I'm going to call you Daphne.

DAANYA. Daanya, sir.

ONE. Now, Daphne:
What are you doing here?

DAANYA. Sir,

I have a good arm, and safe hands,
And I have yet to let a wicket fall

ONE. What?

DAANYA. I'm here to try out for your team, sir.

ONE. My team?

DAANYA. Cricket team. The Lords.

ONE. You came to try out for The Lords?

DAANYA. Yes.

> ONE *scoffs. He looks to* TWO *for solidarity.*
>
> TWO *looks uncomfortable.*

ONE. You came to try out for the team!

DAANYA. I did.
I promise I can bowl better than most of the men on your team,
Just wait and see,
I'm an excellent wicket keeper too,
And you don't have one.

ONE. Why on earth:
Why on Earth
Would you think this is a possibility?

DAANYA. I said, sir.
I'm an excellent bowler.
Best of anyone I've played so far.
And —

ONE. You're a girl!

DAANYA. Yes, sir.

ONE. Have you ever seen a girl on my team?

DAANYA. No, sir, but —

ONE. Have you ever seen a girl playing for Lords?

DAANYA. No, sir, but —

ONE. You're a girl!

This is a waste of my —
Abhi!

DAANYA. Let me bowl for you.

ONE. What makes you think I'd let a girl on my team
Let alone a a a a a a

DAANYA. An Indian

ONE. Girl, yes, on my team?

DAANYA. I thought you might be able to make an exception.

ONE. And why is that?

DAANYA looks at TWO.

TWO *looks sheepish.*

She points at him.

DAANYA. Because of him, sir.

ONE. What him?

DAANYA. Him sir.

ONE. Him?

DAANYA. Yes, sir.

ONE. What about him?

DAANYA looks at TWO *expectantly.*

TWO *looks at his feet.*

DAANYA. I'm his daughter.

ONE. You're —

DAANYA. His daughter.

Pause.

ONE. Well.
Shit.

Pause.

Really?

TWO. Yes.

ONE. Well.

DAANYA. Yes.

ONE. Ah.

TWO. Yes.

ONE. Still.
  I can't make an exception.

DAANYA. Sir,

TWO. But what about —

ONE. No!

DAANYA. He said —

ONE. No!

TWO. Not one teeny-tiny exception?

ONE. No!
  What?
  No! I can't —
  That would be ridiculous
  That would be —
  Why on earth did you make her think this might be possible?

TWO. Throes of passion

ONE. She's your daughter!

TWO. Not with her —
  The mother.

ONE. No!
  Anyway we
  We aren't having trials!
  We aren't having trials.

TWO. Ah.

DAANYA. Look, I know you can't put me in the team.
  I get it.

At least let me train with you.
I train with you, here,
And I can take that training back to my team.

ONE. Your <u>team</u>?

DAANYA. My team

ONE. You have a team.

DAANYA. Yes sir.

ONE. And what would be the <u>point</u> of training you with my team?
What's in it for me?

DAANYA. I'm very good sir.

ONE. Oh are you.

DAANYA. Yes sir. I'll push you, challenge you.

ONE. You think she's good?

TWO. Couldn't really say —

ONE. Alright then.

TWO. What?

ONE. Alright then.
    Show me.

DAANYA. Show you?

ONE. Yes go on. Bowl for me.

DAANYA. Alright sir.

ONE. If you're really that good.

DAANYA. I am.

ONE. Go on.

   DAANYA *paces the space. She takes a run-up.*
   She bowls.
   It's a great ball. Perfect.
   Clear and straight across the stage, flying offstage.

ONE. Well.

DAANYA. Well?

ONE. Do it again.

She does it again.

Pause.

Fine.

TWO. Fine?

DAANYA. Fine?

ONE. Yes.

TWO. What!

ONE. You can train with the team.

DAANYA. Brilliant

ONE. However

DAANYA. Yes?

Pause.

ONE. You must tell me one thing

DAANYA. What sir?

ONE. Where did you get that mango?

DAANYA. Sir?

ONE. That mango, where did you get it?

DAANYA. I

ONE. Where

DAANYA. I can't say.

ONE. What?

DAANYA. Found it

ONE. No you didn't.

DAANYA. Sir, I

ONE. Because Abhi tells me we're out of mangoes.

DAANYA. Well he's

ONE. <u>Abhi tells me we're out of most things</u>

DAANYA. Yes there's no —

ONE. And the tax is owed to us one way or the other
So where did you get it?

DAANYA *looks at* TWO.

TWO *looks at his shoes*.

DAANYA. I

ONE. Because if it exists, the company should get the tax

DAANYA. But

ONE. And you?

TWO. I don't know, I

ONE. Abhi!

DAANYA. I just found it, sir, I did

ONE. Abhi!

TWO. She could have found it on the way she could have
picked it up —

ONE. Abhi!
Where is he?
<u>ABHI</u>!

DAANYA. In my village sir.
On the outskirts of the town.
We.
We have a tree.

ONE. Oh you <u>have a tree do you</u>?

DAANYA. Not many sir.

ONE. Tree<u>s</u>?

DAANYA. Barely any considering —

ONE. How many?

DAANYA. I couldn't say —

ONE. How many?

DAANYA. One, just one

ONE. You knew about this?

TWO. I

ONE. You knew about this?

TWO. It's a bad tree

DAANYA. Tiny.

ONE. And the tax?
Bring the ledger.

TWO. No, no need to —

ONE. Show me that you collected the taxes for the owner of
this 'tree'
Show me!

TWO. I —

ONE. Abhi!
Where is he?
Abhi!

ABHI *enters*.

Go on then, bring the ledger!

ABHI *exits*.

TWO. It's —

DAANYA. He didn't sir.

Pause.

He spared us the taxes.

ONE. Spared?

TWO. I couldn't have them telling anyone I
Sir, my wife!

ONE. So you <u>paid them off</u>

TWO. No I —

ONE. Yes you <u>paid</u> them <u>off</u> —
Wasting money,

Money that <u>belongs</u> to us
To the <u>company</u>
To <u>me</u>
And you spared them from paying so that —

TWO. Yes I did.
That money buys silence —

ONE. So you get silence and a fuck while I get —

TWO. Yes.

ONE. And now here she is.

TWO. Yes.

    ABHI *enters looking worried*

ONE. And where were you!

ABHI. Sir, there's a —

    MEMSAHIB *stumbles in in her undergarments.*

MEMSAHIB. Don't worry everyone I'm here!

ABHI. Problem inside.

MEMSAHIB. The delegation is coming, have you seen them?
Must look good, must look proper!

ONE. Dahling! What on —

DAANYA. What's wrong with her?

ONE. Go back inside!

MEMSAHIB. Welcome to glow tutorials with Max Factor

DAANYA. Opium?

ABHI. A lot.

TWO. Oh my

MEMSAHIB. I show you how, the line that you want
Is from the top of your ear,
The cheekbones
The bridge of the nose and the forehead

> Making certain that
> I don't look so much
> Fucking like my self
> So I have a natural radiance
> And a natural glow
> Golden glow like gold

ABHI. Memsahib —

MEMSAHIB. Oh Abhi,
> I'm delighted for you.

ONE. What

ABHI. Memsahib?

MEMSAHIB. I'm delighted for you I'm delighted: look at her,
> What a splendid nuptial to witness!

ABHI. Oh, no no no this is just a peasant girl from over the
> wall —

MEMSAHIB. She has a natural glow!

DAANYA. Thank you.

MEMSAHIB. I would like to have a wife

DAANYA/ONE. I'm not his wife! / What!

MEMSAHIB. Too, wives and lands,
> I would like to take
> I would like to take something beautiful and make it mine —
> <u>Wiving</u>

DAANYA. Somebody get her some water, we need to —

TWO. Don't touch her!

> DAANYA *moves towards the* MEMSAHIB.

> ABHI *stops her.*

MEMSAHIB. Do you like it?
> It's made from cow's hoofs yes
> It's what the French do
> They also have cats

I would like to own nature
I would like to own nature like that
Cats
Own it all, nature
But we mustn't repeat ourselves mustn't make the same
mistakes twice!

DAANYA. Do something!

MEMSAHIB. I'll tell you a secret, here in my side there's
a lump,
I'm going to lightly keep growing it out keep gorging
Because why stop why ever stop —

DAANYA *slaps her hard.*

ONE/TWO. Oh / My

MEMSAHIB *falls.*

MEMSAHIB. Oh!

Pause.

DAANYA *kisses her, softly, gently, on the mouth.*

A delicate, soft moment.

DAANYA. Okay?

Pause.

MEMSAHIB *smiles.*

ONE *and* TWO *stand in shock.*

ABHI. Memsahib —

MEMSAHIB. I imagine it as I imagine my face
Arriving on the ship
Pale as the moon as they say and seeing before me
A shadow of mankind all around me
Contoured down the sides of my face,
And my boat comes closer and closer,
Vast sails billowing making clouds next to clouds
And a woman on the shore
She closes her mouth and swallows,
Thinking it must be a dry mouth

Or a fly that flew in
But she opens it again,
And breathes
And looks worried
She sees the darkness sailing in, billowing there on the waves
There's a small boy on the shore and he says
'Ma,' he says, 'what is it?
Do you want me to go to bed?'
And she opens and closes her mouth.
And no words come out.
No words can come out.
And that's how, that's just how.
Prime routines and things like that
Things that don't change so much.
We don't want our contours
The lines we've drawn
The lines we've created here
The lines we gouged into earth
To run away on us —

ONE. Enough!! Enough!

ABHI. Sir she's —

ONE. Enough!

MEMSAHIB. Thank you for listening.

She gets back up.

Noblesse oblige.

She takes DAANYA*'s hand and kisses it.*

ONE. Oh dear god not again!

ONE *rushes towards her and pulls her away from* DAANYA.

TWO. I fear your wife's gone mad

ONE. Help me!

TWO *rushes to help* ONE.

TWO. Dear god!

ONE. No Not <u>You</u>, <u>Abhi</u>!

ABHI *doesn't move.*

Abhi help me!

ABHI *stands still.*

MEMSAHIB. We must all go now!

ONE *and* TWO *drag the* MEMSAHIB *offstage.*

Let me go

MEMSAHIB *screams.*

ONE. For fuck's sake

MEMSAHIB. Let me go

She continues to scream as ONE *and* TWO *drag her, violently, kicking and screaming, offstage.*

Let me go
Let me go
Let me go
Let me go

They exit.

Pause.

ONE *and* TWO *return.*

ONE. Madness!

TWO. Quite!

ONE. Explain, Abhi!

ABHI. Sir, I warned you that was —

A flourish offstage.
MESSENGER *enters.*
He is tired, once well dressed – now worn, and carrying a large rifle across his back.
He stands and stares at them.
They stare at him.
Long pause.

MESSENGER. I come from Bangalore.

ONE. Ah!

The delegation!

ONE *and* TWO *bow and curtsy.*

TWO. You made it!
Great.

MESSENGER. Yes.

ONE. Welcome, welcome!
You find us is a <u>strange situation</u>, but nevermind,
Where is all the rest of your party?
And where are your things, your camels, your servants?

TWO. Surely the Sultan did not send you alone?

MESSENGER. If only you knew what I have seen.
But my darkest fear, is that you <u>do</u> know.
We travelled for days and nights, many weeks.
We left Bangalore a merry party,
Looking forward to our time spent here with you.
But your Bengal is terrifying to behold.
I cannot tell which is worse —
The signs, the first omens
I saw from my window at home each morning back in
Bangalore
And thought nothing of,
Or the sickening sights that have been pressed upon me along
this road.
The streets in Calcutta here today.
Just outside.
We left Bangalore,
And to the foothills of the Eastern Ghats we traveled,
Myself, two others sent from the Sultan,
Three servants who cooked for us along the way,
And the son of my brother, hoping for employment
In the East India Company, here with you.
We wound our way up towards Benares, into Company
territory,
Finally following the Ganga on down into Bengal.
But by the foothills of the Ghats,
We already sent my young nephew back home,

Turned around with one of the servants,
For at each village we saw hunger so deep
We could not look away, and had given over so many of our
provisions,
We knew we would not make the journey with all our
company.
And he being youngest was already weak with some
sickness,
Of the heart or mind or body – it hardly matters.
Whether my nephew made it back to Bangalore I know not.
When we reached Benares,
The point at which we had hoped to get more supplies, fill up
the wagons,
Before we continued on,
The devastation we saw there shook up our already angry
souls,
We spent our last gold, documented the suffering, and
promised we would return again with more food, some good
news.
We left there thinking: Surely this is the worst of it?
Surely this is it?
Oh but it is not.
Benares was merely the first point at which we truly
understood the devastation
That your crop failures have enforced upon our land.
In that city near the great Ganga,
I watched scores of people each morning
Carrying their dead from the homes, from the streets,
And throwing them into the river.
Have you realised, that across the territory you now control,
Rice costs at least twelve times the regular amount,
None can afford that and even if they could,
In most towns it is not available at all.
Those are the streets, and fields, and alleys and hills that you
That your company has devised.
Meanwhile, when passing the Bay of Bengal we saw
East India employees loading the entire contents of the
Bengal treasury into fleets of waiting boats
To be punted down the Ganga to come here.

Each farm we came across I hoped —
Prayed that I would see rice, grain to feed the people,
But instead, instead in every field you have planted
Indigo for dye, poppies for opium.
Believe me, there have been times I thought I could live only
for opium.
Perhaps in times like these, you can.
Famine rushes like a wave across this land, swallows it all,
This land well known for bountiful harvest.
It is not the land that cannot feed its people.
I have loved this land all my life.
In these short years that you have governed,
The end of time seems to have come.
You have pillaged Bengal.
And for what?

Pause.

ONE. For England.

Pause.

Of course.

Pause.

Poor man. What a tale!

TWO. There's really nothing here to worry about!

ONE. You must be having hallucinations —
If the <u>peasants</u> cannot <u>feed themselves</u> through this long
summer,
It's got nothing to do with our company.

TWO. Not at all! We're here to trade

ONE. We're here to help!

TWO. Indeed. Rest here – we've a room prepared.
In the morning you can breakfast with us,
And we will begin the negotiations intended by your Sultan.

ONE. No need to halt business on account of a rough trip!

MESSENGER. No, thank you.
I have delivered the only news that now seems relevant to

give.

I lost those papers from the Sultan anyway.

I'm so tired of all this.

Of history.

Of the weight of it.

The repetition. The déjà vu the sense of doing the same thing again and again and,

I cannot be disappointed again.

I take my leave of you.

I take my leave of all this.

I hope you do the same.

MESSENGER *shoots the rifle into the air, a LOUD bang.*

ONE *and* TWO *shriek.*

MESSENGER *exits.*

ABHI *runs after him.*

Long pause.

Then, ABHI *re-enters slowly, carrying the rifle.*

ONE. Abhi?
    What did you do?

ABHI. Took the rifle that that man handed me.

ONE. Well give it here.

ABHI. No.

ONE. No?

ABHI. You have your own weapons.
    I'll have this one.

TWO. I beg your pardon?

ABHI. I heard everything he said,
    Every true word.
    It's time someone told this story back to you.

TWO. Abhi,
    Be careful what you do

ONE. You make one wrong move

And twenty thousand men will move for me.
Is that what you want?

ABHI. Yes, that's all the reason I need.

ONE. What reason?

ABHI. You have an <u>army</u>.
And you aren't a government
You're a corporation!

ONE. We don't have an <u>army</u>

ABHI. You have armed forces

ONE. <u>En</u>forcing the rules

ABHI. The rules by which you now govern <u>our</u> land

TWO. The rules by which we <u>trade</u>
It's very different, Abhi
It's business

ABHI. Is it? Business? Is all this business?

TWO. Yes

ABHI. Then let's talk business:
This famine that you created,
Millions of pounds in taxes owed,
Taxes that our people cannot pay.
There's no way you're recouping on that debt.

ONE. There is <u>NO</u> debt —

ABHI. I looked at your ledgers.
I know your books.
They're not balanced.
There's no way your crown can bail you out of this

TWO. They already have!

ABHI. What?

TWO. The bailout

ONE. Has already begun!

TWO. All of it.
Money makes the world go round.

ABHI. They can bail you out.
   It's all coming from the same pot.

ONE. Abhi —

ABHI. But there are always consequences,
   This debt will come back round,
   There is blood, blood stained into your very souls,
   It's not going to wash away.
   You've lost.

   ABHI *lifts the rifle*

ONE. Abhi! Enough I

ABHI. This is a match

TWO. Abhi —

ABHI. And I understand the rules.

ONE. Enough!

ABHI. And we're going to win.

   ABHI *cocks the rifle.*

ONE. No!
   I am the winner!
   I am the winner!
   I am the winner!
   I am the winner!
   I am the winner!
   I am the winner!
   I have to be the fucking winner!

   He pulls out a pistol and shoots at ABHI.

   ABHI *leaps to the ground.*

   DAANYA *pulls out a cricket ball and hurls it at* ONE*'s head.*

   DAANYA*'s ball is a perfect hit.*

   ONE *falls, dead.*

   DAANYA *takes out a second ball.*

   TWO *rushes towards* ABHI*'s rifle.*

DAANYA *raises her arm, holding a second ball, checkmate.*
TWO *freezes.*

TWO *and* DAANYA *stare at each other.*

And stare.

DAANYA*'s arm raised.*
A moment like this and then
ABHI *gets up.*
The fort starts to crack and fall, in a heartbeat, a second,
A bright light over everything, everyone, perhaps the
audience too, is exposed,
And perhaps INDIA 1 *enters, or we catch a glimpse of her.*
And perhaps ENG 1, ENG **2**, *as for a brief second present*
and past
collapse.

DAANYA *throws the ball to* ABHI. *Then perhaps the others*
join too.

The ball flies from one to the other and then

INDIA 1. It's stopped. We're going back on. Let's go.

And then ABHI *tosses the ball into the air and —*

ABHI. Blackout.

Blackout.

A Nick Hern Book

Testmatch first published in Great Britain as a paperback original in 2024 by Nick Hern Books Limited, The Glasshouse, 49a Goldhawk Road, London W12 8QP, in association with Orange Tree Theatre, ETT and Octagon Theatre, Bolton

Testmatch copyright © 2024 Kate Attwell

Kate Attwell has asserted her right to be identified as the author of this work

Cover photography by Rebecca Need-Menear

Designed and typeset by Nick Hern Books, London
Printed in Great Britain by Mimeo Ltd, Huntingdon, Cambridgeshire PE29 6XX

A CIP catalogue record for this book is available from the British Library

ISBN 978 1 83904 352 9

www.nickhernbooks.co.uk/environmental-policy

www.nickhernbooks.co.uk

facebook.com/nickhernbooks

twitter.com/nickhernbooks